*This book is dedicated to
heart-to-heart love
that gives us the
power to harmonize
our individual human differences—
and enables us to create
happy and fulfilling
lives together.*

Contents

A Note to You From the Author   x

I Seven Guidelines for Going Into a Relationship

1 Understand the Meaning and Importance of Unconditional Love.   2

2 Develop a Relationship With Yourself Before Getting Deeply Involved With Anyone Else.   12

3 Learn How Your Demands and Preferences Create Your World.   22

4 Be Aware That Falling in Love Is Not a Basis for Commitment.   36

5 Can You Share Life Together in a Way That Contributes to Your Mutual Well-Being?   42

6 Honor Your Differences.   52

7 Don't Expect the Relationship to Make You Happy.   58

II Seven Guidelines for Creating a Delightful Relationship

8 Communicate Deeper and Deeper Levels of Honesty.   74

9 Ask for What You Want, but Don't Be Addicted to Getting It.   88

10 Work on Your Own Personal Growth— Not Your Partner's.   94

11 Notice That Both You and Your Partner Always Have Beneficial, Positive Intentions.   104

12 Give All the "Gifts" You Can Emotionally Afford to Give.   118

13 Discover How Your Relationship Is Perfect for Your Enjoyment or Growth.   122

14 Enrich Your Relationship by Helping Others.   130

What People Are Saying About
The Power of Unconditional Love

"*The Power of Unconditional Love* is a gift from Ken Keyes, Jr. I know him personally and see him modeling the love he speaks about. This book is practical and specific. You can use it to begin enriching your relationships immediately."

John Bradshaw
Author, *John Bradshaw On: The Family*
and *Healing the Shame That Binds You*

"Ken Keyes' book *The Power of Unconditional Love* is a marvelous source of deep insight expressed in simple language with clarifying examples. It is one of the most accessible sources of wisdom I have ever found."

Willis Harman
President, Institute of Noetic Sciences
Author, *Global Mind Change*

"*The Power of Unconditional Love* gives practical and pragmatic ways to open your heart to love. It can help you transform your marriage, your work, and your relationship with yourself—your entire life."

Gerald G. Jampolsky, M.D.
Author, *Love Is Letting Go of Fear*
Founder, Center for Attitudinal Healing

"Ken Keyes' books convey profound wisdom and make it practical with elegant simplicity."

Deepak Chopra, M.D.
Author, *Quantum Healing and Perfect Health:*
The Complete Mind/Body Guide

"Your books have made an enormous difference in the quality of life on this planet and your love has reached into all of our hearts."

Terry Cole-Whittaker
Author, *How to Have More in a Have-Not World*
and *What You Think of Me Is None of My Business*

"The miracle of recovery and healing is available to all those who make choices. Ken Keyes, Jr. gives us important and clear direction for how to make those choices."

Sharon Wegscheider-Cruse
Author, *Choicemaking: For Co-Dependents,
Adult Children and Spirituality Seekers*

"*The Power of Unconditional Love* is a practical guide to understanding and facilitating one's ability to accept, care for, and feel warmly toward other human beings. Ken and Penny Keyes realize that this wisdom is hard to come by in our culture. Their advice, if followed, will improve the reader's relationships with others, enabling them to open their hearts as well as their minds."

Stanley Krippner, Ph.D.
Professor of Psychology
Coauthor, *Personal Mythology* and *Healing State*

"I have read and learned from the teachings of Ken Keyes for fifteen years and feel *The Power of Unconditional Love* is the masterwork of his twelve books in print."

Don H. Parker, Ph.D.
Educational Psychologist
Publications used in 61 countries

"You have made such a tremendous contribution in your efforts to awaken people to how important love is."

Ann Wigmore
Ann Wigmore Institute for Research
Boston, Massachusetts

"The insights in *The Power of Unconditional Love* offer urgently relevant guidelines for personal fulfillment. They also provide guidelines for national societies in an interdependent world in which the histories of people of diverse cultures and world views are intersecting in a common future."

Gerald F. Mische, Ph.D.
President, Global Education Associates
Associates in over 80 countries

"Ken Keyes' books are major contributions to a sorely-needed science of love."

Robert Muller
Former U.N. Assistant Secretary-General
Author, *Most of All They Taught Me Happiness*

"*The Power of Unconditional Love* presents a needed bridge that leads us from the shadows of our pain to appreciating and loving ourselves—and others. It gives us guidelines for understanding and accepting our personal struggles so we can then find intimacy by sharing all of ourselves in our wholeness. I admire your courage in showing how to terminate a relationship (if needed) while honoring the integrity of both people."

Allen (Kip) Flock, M.S.W.
Clinical Director, Life Plus Treatment Center
for Co-Dependency

"We seek many substitutes for love—shopping, working constantly, getting ahead—which result in binding addictions and emptiness. *The Power of Unconditional Love* shows us a better way—how to remove the barriers to love and how to open our lives to let it in. The process in the 21 guidelines will allow anyone to feel deeply loved. Wonderful!"

Don Tilley, Ph.D.
Founder, World Peace Center
Lincoln, Nebraska

"Your new book, *The Power of Unconditional Love*, is a handbook for using the only power that matters, the power of love. It may help us all to learn that Love is an energy, not just an emotion."

Paul Solomon
Founder, Fellowship of the Inner Light
Virginia Beach, Virginia

"*The Power of Unconditional Love* really makes sense. I recommend the book highly for any of us wanting to deepen our relationship with a partner."

Roger W. Axford, Ph.D.
Professor of Adult Education
Arizona State University

The Power of Unconditional Love:

21 Guidelines for Beginning, Improving, and Changing Your Most Meaningful Relationships

Ken Keyes, Jr.
with Penny Keyes

LOVE LINE BOOKS
Coos Bay, Oregon 97420

Your purchase of any Love Line book helps to build a more loving and caring world. Royalties are used by a non-profit organization dedicated to teaching Living Love and the Science of Happiness.

The Power of Unconditional Love: 21 Guidelines for Beginning, Improving, and Changing Your Most Meaningful Relationships may be obtained through your local bookstore, or you may order it from the Ken Keyes College Bookroom, 790 Commercial Ave., Coos Bay, OR 97420 for $7.95 plus $1.50 for postage and handling.

Total in print 305,000
Printed on long-lasting acid-free paper

This is an extensive revision of
A Conscious Person's Guide to Relationships.

Library of Congress Cataloging-in-Publication Data
Keyes, Ken.
    The power of unconditional love : 21 guidelines for beginning, improving, and changing your most meaningful relationships / Ken Keyes, Jr., with Penny Keyes.
-- Rev. 3rd ed.
    p.   cm.
    ISBN 0-915972-19-0
    1. Love. 2. Intimacy (Psychology). 3. Interpersonal relationships. I. Keyes, Penny. II. Title.
BF575.L8K496 1990   89-13165
158'.2--dc20   CIP

LOVE LINE BOOKS
700 Commercial Avenue
Coos Bay, OR 97420

III *Seven Guidelines for Altering Your Involvement*

15 For Your Own Growth, Consider Staying Involved Until You Have Changed Your Demands to Preferences. 140

16 Alter Your Involvement If You No Longer Want to Cooperate in the Great Adventure of Life. 144

17 Take Responsibility for Altering the Relationship—and Don't Blame Yourself or Your Partner. 148

18 Be Totally Open and Don't Lie or Hide Things. 154

19 Follow Through on Your Commitments or Work Out a Change in the Commitments. 160

20 Hold On to Heartfelt Love, for Only This Will Enable You to Make Wise Decisions. 164

21 It's Only a Melodrama—So Don't Get Caught Up in It. 170

IV *Loving Unconditionally*

22 Reflections on Love. 180

23 Learning to Love. 184

V *Messages*

Acknowledgments 194

Workshops for Personal Growth 195

Other Books by Ken 197

Index 207

ix

A Note to You
From the Author

I wrote this book to offer you dynamic techniques for personal growth that have empowered me to create a fulfilling, happy life. You will learn how unconditional love can help you achieve what you're really looking for in your life. How-to-do-it information is woven into all the chapters.

I also have a second purpose in writing this book. It is to specifically show how you can use these skills in developing a deeply satisfying relationship with a partner with whom you choose to share your life. Thus I hope you will reap a double enrichment from the time you spend absorbing its practical guidelines.

Part One of this book contains seven guidelines to help you prepare yourself for a relationship that can fulfill your heart's desire for love and intimacy. Part Two explains seven additional guidelines that can make your relationship richer and more delightful when you have chosen your partner. It is directed toward relationships that have the deeper involvement of marriage—but the guidelines are universally applicable to lovers, children, brothers, sisters, parents, in-laws, friends, bosses, employees, and so forth. All the 14 guidelines in Parts One and Two can help you increase your ability to make your present relationship work through the enormous power of unconditional love.

I would like to say that if you read this book, you will live happily ever after. But this would be a lie, and lies are not helpful in getting the most from our lives. So-o-o-o, life being the way it is, in case the relationship doesn't work out, this book contains seven guidelines for altering your involvement in a relationship—another way of saying, "We aren't together anymore." And it shows how to hold on to love in your heart in this challenging situation.

The "Aha" Experience

Some years ago, one of our staff members left for several months to study with another teacher. When she came back, her face was radiant. She told me that she had learned something very important and that it was making a large difference in her life. I was quite curious. What could this teacher be imparting that was so vital? So I asked her what it was she had learned. Her eyes lit up as she exclaimed, "He told me to love everyone!"

I was astounded. Over and over (almost *ad nauseam*) I tell people in my books to love everyone unconditionally. I've even tried to emphasize it by calling it the "law" of higher consciousness: "Love Everyone Unconditionally—Including Yourself." I knew she had read my books. How could this have remained a secret to her?

Some of the things that we need to learn in our personal growth are what might be called "self-secret." Some ideas cannot be taught—they have to be caught. Psychologists call it the "aha" experience.

Somehow this person was able to tell her to "love everyone" in a way that happened to fit her particular programming. Whatever it was, he tossed it to her in a way that enabled her to catch it—to really hear it. This may be what poet Robert Frost meant when he wrote, "I am not a teacher, but an awakener."

Some of the guidelines in this book are mentioned over and over again. If a person is interested only in the intellectual content, this repetition may seem unnecessary. However, if you want to apply these guidelines in your life, their repetition in different contexts may increase your opportunity to turn on that "light bulb" in your mind.

Stretching Our Language

Penny, as a fine editor and proofreader, and I, as an author, want to write in a nonsexist way. English today lacks singular third person common gender pronouns. We're not willing to bog down the reader with, "When you hide your real feelings from your partner, you're depriving him or her of the realities of life she or he needs to work on himself or herself to go beyond her or his demanding programming." Since third person plural pronouns in English are not gender-specific, we've decided to use "them," "they," "themselves," and "their" for both singular and plural. Thus it will come out, "When you hide your real feelings from your partner, you're depriving them of the realities of life they need to work on themselves to go beyond their programming." We hope it reads smoothly.

Needed Repair Work

These guidelines can be useful to everyone in their journey of personal growth. However, individuals who need a lot of repair work in dysfunctional inner child or codependent areas should get additional help. Unfortunately pain from the past may unknowingly block their hearts—for now. Perhaps the vision of what life can be as presented in this book may lead them to seek needed counseling.

I hope you will find this book illuminating and inspiring. Penny and I send you our love, encouragement, and best wishes for bringing the power of unconditional love into your life.

Ken Keyes, Jr.
Coos Bay, Oregon

PART I

Seven Guidelines for Going Into a Relationship

1

Understand the Meaning and Importance of Unconditional Love.

Most people don't understand unconditional love. A popular writer recently wrote that unconditional love means "indifference" to your partner's actions. He thought that unconditional love requires that you go along with everything a person does! Most people are stuck in this mistake. This popular error kills your ability to even understand "unconditional love"—much less discover how to bring its vital power into your life.

Even after a person has an understanding of what it means, the ego may resist putting it into practice—especially in an intimate relationship. Our egos are tempted to run the clincher, "If you really loved me, you would . . ." (here we fill in what we want from our partner). But real love cannot be used as a baseball bat to get our way.

Here's the key that can open the door to a richer life:

Love Everyone Unconditionally—Including Yourself.

It's not easy to develop the skill of loving unconditionally. So why even try? Why not simply make it OK to love your partner with conditions? "I'll love you if you do what I want." "I don't love you when you. . . ." I used to do just that until I discovered the enjoyment and profound happiness that practicing unconditional love brings me—and my partner. I learned that the degree of happiness I create for myself depends on the amount of unconditional love I maintain in my heart.

What Is Unconditional Love?

Power-oriented people think that a 20-megaton nuclear missile is far more powerful than the force of love. And they're probably right if they're thinking of the most powerful killing force on earth. And they're absolutely wrong if they're talking about the greatest force for living a fulfilling, happy life on this planet.

To bring the power of unconditional love into your life, let's begin by clarifying what we mean by this term. The ancient Greeks had a word for unconditional love: *agape*, which is heart-to-heart love with no strings attached to yank love back if we don't like what someone does. The Greeks also distinguished *agape* from e*ros* (sexual love) and from *philia* (friendship or fraternal love). No wonder we can get confused. In the English language, we have only one word, "love," that points to all these different events.

In learning to love unconditionally, we must first understand what it is that we are loving without conditions. Some people have told me, "I don't *want* to love everyone!" Others have said, "How about people who do horrible things no one could love? I can't love a murderer! So how could I possibly love unconditionally? It can't be done."

And yet it must be done to get the tremendous benefits of unconditional love in your life. And perhaps you're already doing it—sometimes! Have you ever liked a person even though you definitely did not like something the person did or said? *You mentally separated the person from the problem.*

4

The only way I can love unconditionally is to distinguish between a *person* and their *programming*, which causes the person's behavior. And that's what most people don't know how to do.

You Are Not Your Tapes

How do we mentally distinguish between a person's behavior and the person? I find it helpful to use an analogy: I have a cassette player. Suppose I play a tape I find awful. Even though I dislike the *tape*, this does not cause me to dislike the *tape player*. My tape player simply played the tape—perfectly. I can dislike the *program* being played—and still like the *player*.

The same is truc of people. People are like the tape player. They are, in their essence, OK just as they are. But they can run off tapes in their minds that make them do things that are unacceptable, unskillful, and harmful to themselves or others.

I can totally reject and even actively oppose what a person is saying and doing. And at the same time, I can continue to *love that person* no matter what their behavior is. My ego just has to let me remember that the person is *not* the mental tapes (conditioning, habits of mind, or *programming*) they have learned.

An example of unconditional love is a mother's love for her young child. She can love her child when he comes into the house covered with mud and tracks it over the recently mopped floor. She can love him when he jumps on the couch after she has told him to clean up in the bathtub. And she can even love him when he yells, "No! I won't!" and she has to pick him up and carry him into the bathroom while he's kicking and screaming.

She's completely opposed to his *behavior* and doesn't like *that* at all. And yet she still loves *him*. She doesn't confuse the tape player with the tape that is being played out!

It is often easiest for us to love very young children unconditionally. They are such tiny bundles of cuddly, soft cuteness that pull on our heartstrings. It is a much greater challenge to apply this to our relationship partner. The multifaceted involvement of living together brings out demanding programming we never knew we had!

Yet if we learn to recognize the programs we don't like as just mental habits we picked up, we can learn to go beyond them and love unconditionally. Our partner is not the "tapes" or the programs they have learned. And unconditional love does not tie our hands. We can still strongly dislike, and even oppose, what that person does. I will keep repeating this because most people's ego makes them forget it when they most need to remember it.

There is another reason why I find it helpful to avoid lumping together the tape player and a particular tape or programming I don't like. Our minds are more than tape players—they're also tape *recorders*. That means we can make new tapes—or we can *reprogram* tapes that don't work well. We have the capability of putting in any program we want!

Unconditional Love in Relationships

While I've never thrown away a tape recorder just because I didn't like the program it was playing, I unfortunately have thrown people out of my heart because I didn't like the tape or program their minds were

6

using. *I forgot that we human beings are not our programming!*

Are you beginning to get accustomed to using the word "programming" to refer to a way of thinking or reacting that a person has learned? We are basically good; our programming can sometimes cause problems. Computer buffs use the saying "Garbage in, garbage out." In our essence, we are OK. And garbage mental habits can trash our lives.

Now that we're beginning to understand what we mean by unconditional love, we can learn why it is an essential ingredient for heart-to-heart relationships. To begin with, we are certain to find things about our partner that we want different. Conflicts may come up occasionally, frequently, or continuously. If we cloud our minds with fear, frustration, resentment, anger, and a "me-*vs.*-you" hostility, the options that occur to us for resolving disagreements will be limited. Unconditional love opens up our options.

For example, suppose Kate and Wilbur agreed to deposit $100 per month from each of their paychecks in a vacation account. Let's say Kate doesn't make the quota each month because she keeps collecting antique clocks (which Wilbur regards as house-cluttering junk). Wilbur has repeatedly reminded her of their agreement to save $100 a month. Kate promises she will start "next month." She has been saying this for five months.

Wilbur originally started out reminding Kate of her obligation in a matter-of-fact way. But now he's beginning to feel resentful that she is not keeping her agreement. As the months go by, Wilbur brings up the issue, expressing more and more feelings of anger and resentment. One day he blows up and yells at Kate, "You make me mad! You are irresponsible!"

In this moment, he doesn't feel any love for Kate. Wilbur is thinking about what it would be like to take a vacation without her—and perhaps meet someone who would appreciate him—since Kate surely doesn't! He also feels exhausted from the emotional strain he's been putting himself through worrying about this. Kate responds by refusing to speak to Wilbur for a week. A dark cloud now hangs over their relationship.

Opening the Heart to Love

Now let's turn the clock back and replay this scenario. Suppose Wilbur knew about the power of unconditional love. He reminds Kate of her agreement. Kate doesn't save for the vacation budget. Wilbur tells himself that Kate has programming he does not like. And he knows that Kate is much more than her programs—just as a tape player is much more than the particular program it is playing.

He wants her to keep her agreement. He also knows he wants to keep loving Kate unconditionally. He can't control Kate, but he can learn to control his demanding *reaction* to the situation. He can use this situation to practice distinguishing between this small part of Kate's programming (which he doesn't love) and Kate (whom he does love).

Unconditional love means learning to separate the person from the problem. Love the person; work with the problem.

So now as Wilbur approaches Kate about their agreement, he remembers that she is not the behavior she is acting out—she is not her tapes. She is a

8

beautiful human being whom he loves. Now he can more easily remain calm, feel love for her, and still try to change her programmed behavior. Wilbur tells her, "I love you, and I don't like it when you don't keep your agreement to save $100 a month for our vacation." He's not yelling at her. He doesn't accuse her of making him unhappy. (In Chapter 3 you'll discover that no one can make you unhappy!)

Kate may not feel so threatened or attacked by Wilbur because she senses his love for her behind the words. He may want to explore what underlying interests or concerns motivate Kate to keep shortchanging their vacation account after she had agreed to put aside $100 a month. Wilbur's unconditional love may help Kate change.

What if Kate doesn't change? Wilbur definitely has a challenge here. And yet his chances for experiencing life on a happier level are enhanced when he communicates with clarity and love. He feels loving, no matter what happens. He knows that *their love for each other is more important* than a vacation—or almost anything else. If they lose their love, the vacation together will be ruined anyway.

Appreciating and Loving Yourself

Many people have programming that makes them equate self-appreciation and self-love with selfishness and self-centeredness. You may recall the legend of Narcissus, who looked into a pond and fell in love with his own image. And I certainly agree that people who seem interested only in themselves will be deprived of the joy of an emotionally rich relationship.

Our saying *"Love everyone unconditionally— including yourself"* does not suggest this self-centered

9

type of love. Instead, it points toward a self-esteem and self-appreciation that is essential to one's mental health. If you have programming that constantly makes you feel self-doubt, self-rejection, or self-hate, it is vital that you root it out.

We have a friend who at one time was an instructor at our school. It seems that everyone loves Franklin—they instantly gravitate to him and want to be with him. I think it's because he radiates unconditional love and acceptance for others because he loves and accepts himself.

Through inner work you can develop genuine self-confidence, self-acceptance, self-appreciation, and self-respect. Have patience—it takes time.

Empowering Yourself With Love

Anyone who lives without the energy of unconditional love passes through life like a ship dragging its anchor. Dr. Pitirim A. Sorokin (Professor of Sociology at Harvard University from 1930 to 1964 and President of the American Sociological Association from 1965 to 1968) wrote in *The Ways and Power of Love:*

> Unselfish love has enormous creative and therapeutic potentialities, far greater than most people think. Love is a life-giving force, necessary for physical, mental, and moral health.

Research has shown that love in our hearts can enable us to create internal joy and serenity, which make us healthier and able to live longer.* It can put more years in your life—and more life in your years. It is the most powerful force there is for living a fulfilling, peaceful, happy life on this planet.

---

* To better understand the healing power of love, see *Love, Medicine and Miracles* by Dr. Bernie Siegel (Harper & Row, 1986).

Only the power of unconditional love can enable two people to live joyously together. Only the power of unconditional love enables a mother and father to bring new life on earth and *successfully* nurture it during the years of infancy, childhood, and adolescence. And only the power of unconditional love enables two people to create a wonderful trust and comfort with each other's diverse programming, different backgrounds, and changing wants and interests.

If you're already in a relationship, I'm sure life is providing you with plenty of opportunities to practice the enriching guidelines in this book. If you are not presently in a relationship, you can begin preparing now by practicing unconditional love with everyone you come in contact with—including yourself. Then when you enter into a relationship, you will have an enormous advantage. By opening your life to the power of unconditional love, you can enjoy the most fulfilling relationship possible.

2

Develop a Relationship With Yourself Before Getting Deeply Involved With Anyone Else.

Most of us are looking for a relation-*ship* that will carry us securely across the seas of separateness and loneliness to the beautiful shores of love, joy, and happiness. Since divorce statistics show that about half the people who begin the journey are abandoning ship, and the popular jokes about male-female relationships indicate that many married couples are not happy together, it may pay off handsomely to increase our skill in making this voyage. So let's begin at the beginning.

If you tell yourself you must have a relationship to be happy, you're already in trouble. If you are presently in a relationship, you may be undermining it in various ways by demanding and clinging. If you take two dominoes and lean them against each other, you have an unstable setup; if one of them moves, the other falls. If you create the experience that you are only half a person, and you need someone to somehow help you fill in the missing half, you're setting yourself up for a dysfunctional relationship.

Your partner cannot make you feel good or guarantee your self-esteem or self-confidence. Count yourself fortunate if your partner can do this for themselves! Author and lecturer John Bradshaw of the Center for Recovering Families in Houston, Texas tells us, "The goal of life is to move from environmental support to self-support. So what we look at then is the possibility of going deeper within ourselves."[*]

[*] From John Bradshaw's PBS television series. I recommend Bradshaw's revealing book *Bradshaw On: The Family, A Revolutionary Way of Self-Discovery* (Health Communications, Inc., 1988).

13

You may prefer to have a relationship, but you'll make yourself miserable if you demand it. A part of your inner growth will be to develop your own self-confidence, self-acceptance, and self-support.

There was a time when I told myself I needed a female companion in order to be happy. I lived on a boat docked in Miami. When I saw a beautiful sunset alone, I made myself feel hollow. I wanted to share it with someone. Wanting to share is a natural part of being human, but my *insistence* on sharing simply retarded my happiness.

Then I began developing my skill using the guidelines explained in this book. I became aware that I was *addictively demanding* to have a partner. I decided to get free from this program because it was making me unhappy. Was it possible to stop *demanding* that life give me a partner—and at the same time be open to *preferring* a relationship with someone? I had a breakthrough experience that answered this question.

I was on top of a hill watching a sunset. I was alone. Something began to happen. As the sun descended into the ocean and twilight developed, I realized that I had been making myself unhappy with my demand for a companion—and I didn't need to do that any longer. I weighed my choices. An awareness came over me that I could simply let the demand go. The inner work with these guidelines paid off. It became a *preference* to have a partner—but not a requirement for my happiness. From then on I could enjoy my life without longing for a partner, clinging to past memories, or asking fruitless questions about how long I would have to wait before I could find a partner. I was developing my relationship with myself.

I was learning to enjoy what's in my life right now. The idea was sinking in that the now moment is all I ever have. The past is gone. When the future arrives, it will always be now—the eternal now moment!

Preparing for a Satisfying Relationship

A relationship may at first give you the illusion of working smoothly while your separate-self egos are still in hiding. But when both of you eventually relax the facades that conceal your real feelings, you'll find the need for inner work may pop up unexpectedly. Dating, friendships, and work relationships usually don't even get near the deeper levels of expectations—hiding in the *subconscious* part of your mind. Living together can explode these buried bombs. The more you're involved with someone, the more that person will tend to trigger any unfinished business from your childhood. You'll trigger theirs, too.

Dr. Charles Whitfield has pointed out:

> Not everyone was mistreated or abused as a child. No one really knows how many people grow up with a healthy amount and quality of love, guidance and other nurturing. I estimate perhaps 5 to 20%. This means that from 80 to 95% of people did not receive the love, guidance and other nurturing necessary to form consistently healthy relationships, and to feel good about themselves and about what they do.*

Therefore, being in a relationship before you're ready for it may be too hot a fire for you to handle. Give yourself the gift of working through some of the mental habits that keep you from living harmoniously with *yourself*—as well as a partner. You can't do it

* From *Healing the Child Within* by Charles L. Whitfield, M.D. (Health Communications, Inc., Deerfield Beach, Florida, copyright 1987). Reprinted with the permission of the publishers. Highly recommended.

15

all before, but you can get a good start in this direction. Then it will be much easier for you to handle your programming when it clashes with your partner's tapes.

Here's how this was explained in one of our workshops:

> Our guideline suggests that you develop a relationship with yourself before getting involved with another person. I don't mean that unless you totally love yourself you don't get involved in a relationship with anyone else. But I want to warn you that *the inner work necessary on self-acceptance is a lot easier outside of a relationship.* Because a relationship is like a mirror right there at the tip of your nose. It constantly reflects where you're not loving yourself— and it won't go away. Constantly reflecting your stuff. . . . And so you need to be grounded in the methods—to be continually looking at the "programming" that keeps you from loving yourself.*

Dysfunctional Inner Child Programs

Be open to the insight that most of your relationship problems stem from dysfunctional programming you probably picked up in the first few years of your life. Most of us were mistreated emotionally (if not physically) when we were small children. An adult who is acting out their addictive programming can seem very threatening and frightening to a toddler. We carry these traumas with us as we grow up.

Inside most of us are programs that override healthy adult responses to many situations that come up with our partners. "You no longer have the memories," Bradshaw says, "but the repressed emotions form a frozen energy core that *unconsciously runs your life.*"†

* All excerpts from workshops are taken from a Living Love relationship course led by Carole Thompson Lentz.

† Techniques for healing destructive childhood programs are beyond the scope of this book. For ways to heal your "injured child," you may wish to read *Healing the Shame That Binds You* by John Bradshaw (Health Communications, Inc., 1988). This book is helpful even if you don't think there's any shame that binds you. You'll find out there is.

Below the Surface

These dysfunctional programs act like cesspools of infection in the subconscious mind; they are a source of mental illness. They psychosomatically tear at our bodies. And they give a hidden support to many of our demands on our partners and ourselves that we could otherwise change to preferences. Because they operate in the subconscious mind, they are like the 85 percent of a dangerous iceberg that lies concealed under the surface of the sea.

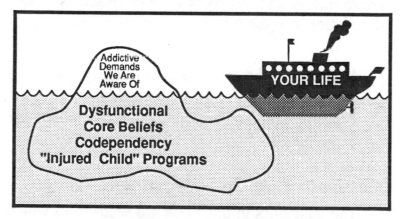

The list of subconscious programs that keep us trapped may be extensive: "No one really loves me." "People I love will leave me." "I'm not good enough." "Men/women can't be trusted." "I don't deserve a good life." "It's dangerous to be attractive." "No matter what I do, it's never good enough." "Other people know better how to run my life." "People won't like me if they really know me." And so forth—on and on into the night.

Your mind may *intellectually* tell you, "I have the right to be me. I'm OK." But sometimes we don't experience ourselves this way in our feelings or emotions. In spite of our realistic rational thoughts, we may still be subconsciously motivated by shame, guilt, self-rejection, emptiness, fear, confusion, burning resentment, self-hatred, or chronic anxiety.

If you grew up in a family with inappropriate or dysfunctional responses, you didn't learn what's appropriate or functional. Psychological warps seem "normal"—until you do some repair work.

You'll need all the insight you can get to meet the emotional challenges of living intimately with another person. When you marry, you marry your partner's whole history. And your partner must live with your entire history. The success of your relationship will depend on your understanding, wisdom, and unconditional love.

> *You are not responsible for the programming you picked up in childhood. However, as an adult, you are 100 percent responsible for fixing it.*

Cultivating the Soil for Growth

The guidelines in this book are seeds from which happiness, inner peace, love, and enjoyment can grow in your life. The "injured child" scars deplete the soil in which these seeds can sprout. If a plant needs alkaline soil, it will be greatly retarded if the soil is acid. Healing your dysfunctional "injured child" scars acts as a dramatic soil conditioner that enables you to enjoy your life to the fullest. So instead of jumping into a complex involvement such as marriage, you may have more fun in the long run if you hold out for a while and work on yourself.

I had to learn this the hard way by putting myself through the wringer of two marriages and two divorces—always blaming my partner for its not working out. Over a decade I gradually built up my skill in applying these relationship guidelines. By focusing on inner personal growth, I learned how to bring the magic of unconditional love into my life. I am now greatly enjoying my third marriage. My marriage with Penny started out happily, and it's more fun year after year.

In the soap opera we call life, I play the part today of a 69-year-old gray-haired cripple who spends his life in a wheelchair. If I can find happiness, so can you. But it takes knowledge, determination, and practice, practice, and more practice in using these growth guidelines.*

Be Gentle With Yourself

It's fine to have ideals and goals. But if you expect instant results and fall short of your perfectionistic striving, you don't have to beat up on yourself. You can't sow and reap the same day. Watch out for any impatient demands that you "should" grow faster.

You can learn to be gentle with yourself and others. You can learn to view a "failure" as a great opportunity to grow. The truth is that most successes are built on a multitude of failures—because we learn from them. As an old adage reminds us, "Wisdom is learned more from failure than from success."

Your personal growth will take a lot of inner work. But is there a better way to invest your energy than to put it into your growth? What you'll get back is the foundation for more happiness for the rest of your life.

---

* There are many books, 12-step groups, and growth centers that may help you discover your inner beauty. If you feel attracted to the Living Love methods for working on yourself, you may wish to deepen your skills by reading my *Handbook to Higher Consciousness* and *Gathering Power Through Insight and Love*. Part V in the back of this book tells where to get Living Love workshops and how-to-do-it books.

Almost everyone self-rejects—some more, some less. And some people reject themselves for rejecting themselves! The psychiatrist Alfred Adler, a disciple of Freud, said that everyone has an inferiority complex—although we may try to cover it up with a mask of superiority.

In childhood you may have believed others when they said you were ugly, stupid, or bad. All this is nonsense, of course. You just handcuffed yourself with the dysfunctional attitudes of people around you. You gave yourself a heavy load of "should's," "should not's," and "ought to's" that kept you telling yourself that you would be lovable if you were different or "better."

No dog would do to itself what you may be doing to yourself. A little dachshund doesn't go around thinking it is inferior because it doesn't have the long legs of a greyhound. Greyhounds don't put themselves down by saying, "I'm a failure. I'd have it made if I were short and cuddly and could sit on someone's lap like a dachshund." They're OK the way they are—and so are you. If you don't feel OK about yourself, the only reason is that both your conscious and subconscious mental habits may be telling you that you have to be different to be OK.

Your programming in some areas may be unskillful—or even harmful—but *in your essence as a human being*, you are always beautiful, capable, and lovable. And you may choose to change some of your programming to enjoy your life more—and get along better with other people. You can give your life a great boost by getting on with your personal growth.

Give Yourself Time for Growth

You don't need another relationship breakup that gives your ego and mind more illusory "evidence" of how inadequate and incapable you are—or how awful your partner is. *You are OK the way you are—and the world has a place for you.* In your essence, you are equal to everyone and everyone is equal to you.

> *If you are creating the illusion that you must have a relationship, you can put damaging pressure on both yourself and the relationship. Don't be in too big a hurry to get involved with someone. Make friends with yourself first.*

And don't leap into a relationship because your ego is afraid someone you like will get away. Remember it is more important to *be* the right person than to *find* the right person!

The guidelines in this book can help you develop a relationship with yourself. And you must practice using them in your daily life situations. It's like learning any skill. Books can tell you how, but only practice builds your effectiveness.

"Of all the people you will know in a lifetime," wrote Jo Coudert in *Advice From a Failure*, "you are the only one you will never leave or lose." You can uncover the beautiful, capable, and lovable you that a part of your programming may be hiding. Start now to practice understanding, acceptance, compassion,* and *unconditional appreciation and love for yourself.* Then let others discover you!

---

* Webster defines compassion as sympathetic consciousness of others' distress together with a desire to alleviate it. I suggest that you also feel compassion for yourself (a gift of your unified-self to your separate-self).

3

Learn How Your Demands and Preferences Create Your World.

It has been said, "Some pursue happiness—others create it." Let's examine how to create it in your daily life—in spite of all the situations and people you blame for making you upset.

I want to introduce the word "demand" (or "addiction" or "addictive demand") so we can use it as a tool for communicating about life. A demand is an insistent requirement. When we use the term "addictive demand," we will be referring to *something we tell ourselves we must have to be happy*. If we don't get our way, we will *automatically* make ourselves feel emotionally upset. By our definition, all demands are addictive, for we insistently require them to let ourselves feel happy.

In other words, an addiction is *an emotion-backed demand, model, or expectation* for how a person or thing "should" or "should not" be. We are all familiar with such statements as "He has a nicotine addiction." Now let's greatly expand our use of this word so that it becomes a useful *tool* in discovering things about ourselves. For example, if I get angry when you keep me waiting, I am addicted to your being on time. My feelings of anger, fear, frustration, or any separating emotions are the tip-off as to whether or not I am addictively demanding.

Thus you can tell whether you have an addiction by your *emotions*. This means going beyond what you tell yourself you *should* be feeling. It means becoming aware of how you *actually feel*—not what you think.

It's your gut-level feelings that help you pinpoint your mind's demanding programs.

People can have addictions about *anything*. Addictive demands can seem petty, silly, unreasonable, impossible, illogical. Yet when you're caught in one, to you it will usually seem justified, sensible, and right.

Each time the world doesn't fit our emotion-backed models of how things should be, each time something or someone triggers one of our demands, our minds automatically create some form of unhappiness. Personal growth involves changing our programming so that our addictive demands are replaced by *preferences*. Then the magic starts!

We can define a preference as *a desire that does not make us feel upset or unhappy if it is not satisfied.* When things happen that we don't like, with preferential programming our minds don't trigger upsetting, separating responses. This gives us more insight, more choice, and more rapport with our partner. Our enjoyment is not dependent on controlling everyone and everything around us. Our lives work much better. And we are happier!

The Cause of Unhappiness

We largely live in our emotions and feelings. We're learning that our feelings of fear and self-confidence, frustration and fulfillment, and anger or joy are created in each moment by our programming as it is stimulated by life events.*

It is your demanding programming that creates your feelings of separateness and unhappiness. It acts like

---

* When we use the term "life event," we are referring to the "objective reality" we pick up through our eyes, ears, nose, touch, and other sensory receptors. "Life event" refers to the way things are unfolding in our changing world. A life event can take place either inside our body or in the world outside our skin.

sand in the gears of life. When your demands aren't satisfied, you automatically trigger irritation, resentment, fear, anger, worry, frustration, jealousy, boredom, etc. Your *demanding mental habits* or *programs* actually cause you to make yourself unhappy—but the demanding ego creates a misleading belief in your mind that your partner is making you unhappy. Addictive demands thus make you create lots of illusions in your life. They keep your feelings in turmoil—and can destroy your happiness.

For example, suppose Jack sometimes comes home from work about an hour late. He is evasive when Janie, his wife, asks him about it. He mumbles things like "I got caught in traffic." One day Janie finds out from a friend that Jack goes to the local bar after work with his business friends. Janie becomes furious. She demands that Jack tell her where he has been at night after work.

By our definition, she has ignited one of her addictive demands. Her body tenses up and she experiences feelings of anger, frustration, and rage. She confronts Jack and blurts out, "You should have told me where you were! You lied to me! How can I ever trust you again? You make me so mad!"

Janie's separating emotions are *directly* caused by her addictive demand that Jack let her know where he was. Jack's actions were only the *indirect cause* or *background factor* in her making herself upset. Although Jack was unskillful when he lied, it was Janie's *addictive demand* that he tell her what he was doing that *directly* made her upset. Jack's behavior (not telling Janie where he was) was an event that stimulated Janie's demanding programming—which then sent a command to the limbic part of her brain to trigger her angry emotions. *Without this program in her mind, she would not feel upset by this situation.* For example, Janie's mental program might even be glad for Jack to come home later if she liked to meditate alone at that time of day.

A frequent error of perception occurs when we are righteously upset. Our egos erroneously tell us we don't have an addictive demand when, "I'm right and they're wrong." Right-wrong, good-bad, and fair-unfair are important value judgments. But don't let those judgments confuse you when you're identifying a demand. The whole world can agree that you're right and the other person is wrong. And if you're emotionally upset, *you're caught in a demand.* Some of the most addictively demanding people in this world are *righteously* right! And it's OK to think you're right. Just don't let your ego distract you from accurately identifying an addictive demand when it occurs.

The Key to Happiness

You create your happiness—or unhappiness. If you say, "You make me angry," you are operating from a common fallacy. *Such statements are always an illusion!* A more accurate statement is, "When you do that, my mind triggers my demanding programming, which automatically stimulates my anger." Although our egos may find this somewhat cumbersome to use in a hot argument, this insight can enable us to enormously increase our happiness!

Notice that when you're caught in the illusion, "You make me angry," you have put your happiness in someone else's hands. You are their victim; they are to blame for your feeling upset. How can you

26

empower yourself to consciously create your own happiness so that it does not depend on others—or on things—being different from the way they are?

Here's how: When you change an addictive demand to a preference, you pluck back your power to feel good. *Preferences never make you upset.* If life satisfies your preference, you can create experiences of enjoyment, fulfillment, happiness, and love. When life doesn't meet your preference, instead of creating unpleasant feelings such as fear, frustration, or anger, you just feel relaxed and aware. You tell yourself, "I can emotionally accept it here and now because it's a preference."

Let's go back to Janie and Jack. Suppose when she finds out about Jack's occasional trips to the local tavern, she still wants him to tell her where he has been. She realizes that it is not effective to get upset and demand that Jack be open with her. She wants to keep the love in her heart.

Imagine that through an internal adjustment she changes her addictive demand to a preference. Now her body feels relaxed and she experiences emotions of acceptance and caring. When she sees Jack she says to him, "I just found out you have been going to the tavern sometimes after work. You don't have to hide that from me. I'd rather you come right home after work. But it's OK. Just let me know where you are in case there's an emergency and I need to reach you." No melodrama—and love continues to enhance their relationship.

Addictions vs. Preferences

When you activate an addictive desire that is not being met, your body carries tension and you feel emotionally upset if the demand is not met. When that same desire is instead preferential, your body is free of tension and you feel neutral to pleasant.

This may be further clarified by the diagram below:

HOW OUR MINDS ACTUALLY WORK

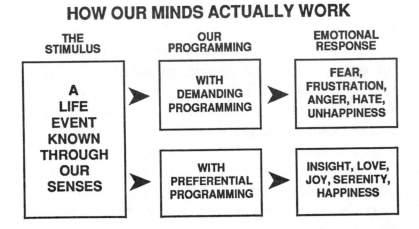

THE STIMULUS	OUR PROGRAMMING	EMOTIONAL RESPONSE
A LIFE EVENT KNOWN THROUGH OUR SENSES	WITH DEMANDING PROGRAMMING	FEAR, FRUSTRATION, ANGER, HATE, UNHAPPINESS
	WITH PREFERENTIAL PROGRAMMING	INSIGHT, LOVE, JOY, SERENITY, HAPPINESS

At first you may have trouble understanding how you could possibly feel relaxed if your preference is *not* met. You can begin by giving yourself credit for having already changed many demands into preferences. Most of the programming in your mind is preferential. Think of all the things you would like to be different and have learned to accept—such as a friend calling at late hours, your boss constantly clicking her fingernails against her pencil, your neighbor not mowing his lawn, or the government taking more taxes from your paycheck than you would like. People who have too many insistent demands can end up committing suicide. And *you're* still here!

As you learn to relate the above diagram to your own life experiences, you will be developing skill in what I call the First Wisdom Principle:

My addictive demands trigger my separating emotions, which create my unhappiness. Preferences never do.

I used to demand that my partner not be periodically depressed and negative. This demand was one of my big issues in my second divorce. Years later I worked on this to alter my addictive programming. As I began to emotionally accept life as it was in each moment, I gave myself an inner peace that my programming had previously prevented when my partner was emotionally upset. I made it OK not to play God and try to control everything in my life. My happiness greatly improved when I discovered that I could *handle my demands* by doing the inner work needed to make them preferences. I began to understand what the sage meant by "The door to the human heart can be opened only from the inside."

Preferences Make Life Work Better

Can you explain what you want to your partner without feeling upset? If so, you probably have a preference. If not, chalk up an addiction.

Remember that a preference is a desire that does not make you upset emotionally if you don't get it. The difference between an addiction and a preference has *nothing* to do with what's happening in your environment. The difference is in your *internal emotional experience.*

Transforming an addiction to a preference doesn't necessarily require a change in your actions, opinions, or models. You can retain all your models of how

29

things "should" be. Just decide if you're tired of making yourself upset, and you really want more love and inner peace. This will nudge your mind to change your demand to a preference.*

> *With a preference you can still think you're right. You can still want things to change. And you can still try to get them to change. The only real difference is that you don't make yourself emotionally upset if you don't get what you want!*

Let's return to Jack and Janie. Janie wants to keep her relationship in harmony, *and* she wants Jack to communicate more openly with her. She has worked on her demand and has changed it to a preference that Jack be open. As a result she asks Jack to spend time with her each evening just before going to bed so they can share what has been happening during the day. She encourages Jack to openly talk with her about his triumphs and failures, his hopes, dreams—and his fears. She is patient when he closes down. Yet she continues to ask him to communicate with her. Janie realizes that with a preference:

- She can still want Jack to tell her where he is after work,
- She can still think Jack should be more communicative,
- She can still ask and encourage Jack to open up to her—
- And she doesn't have to feel angry and upset if she doesn't get what she wants from Jack.

Janie is now more skillful. Her happiness, contentment, and satisfaction are no longer at stake. As a result of her inner work using this guideline, she is not

---

*_Gathering Power Through Insight and Love_ by Penny and myself has additional techniques.

30

playing victim anymore. *She has empowered herself to be the creative cause of her experience!*

Your preferential programming does not make your ego push your emotional alarm buttons. Thus when you use preferences to create your experience of what's here and now in your life, you can *emotionally* accept what is happening in your life—*and* still try to make changes.

What Is "The" Cause?

A fundamental principle of the Science of Happiness is that no one can make you angry or afraid or frustrated or irritated—or happy or joyous or whatever. This flies in the face of our common way of thinking about cause and effect in creating our emotional experiences. Parents often tell their children, "You're upsetting your mother," or "You gave your father a heart attack." Husbands and wives may tell each other, "You make me jealous," or "When you do that you make me happy." Since complete clarity in this matter of cause and effect is vital to bringing the power of unconditional love into your life, let's take a very close look at what causes what.

Suppose Frank strikes Bill in the head. Bill instantly feels anger toward Frank. What was the cause of Bill's anger? Most people would say, "Bill's angry because Frank hit him." Let's explore this notion in depth and ask even further: "What caused Frank to hit Bill? Isn't that getting closer to the *real cause* of Bill's anger?"

Suppose a psychologist answers that Frank was abused by his father as a child and acquired the programming that taught him to hit anyone who strongly opposed him. With this information, we can meaningfully ask, "Then wasn't Frank's abusive childhood the *real cause* of Bill's anger?" It might seem that we have given a profound answer to finding the cause of Bill's anger until someone asks, "Well, why did Frank's father have this programming to pass on to Little Frank?" Let's suppose the psychologist on further investigation points out that Frank's father got it from *his* father. Well, then wasn't Frank's grandfather the *real cause* of Bill's anger for being hit?

We're now getting into a problem that is known as *infinite regress.* Blaming Frank's grandfather doesn't settle anything because someone could then ask, "Well, where did his grandfather get it? And where did his great grandfather get this violent programming? And where did his great great grandfather get it?"

The fact is that whatever happens to you is preceded by certain things that happened earlier. And those things are preceded by things that happened even earlier. So life is a matter of antecedent conditions creating current realities, which in turn will create what happens in the future. We thus see that it is a gross oversimplification to state that Frank caused Bill's anger.

Behavioral scientists who must be precise about cause and effect have learned not to talk about causes. Instead, they inquire *how* things happen—not *why* they happen. So in understanding *how* Bill became angry, we can follow the programming that Frank's great grandfather passed on to Frank's grandfather, who passed it on to Frank's father, who passed it on to Frank—and Frank's programming made him hit Bill, which stimulated Bill's addictive programming to activate a part of the limbic area of his brain that sent out impulses along his parasympathetic nervous system to create the experience we call anger! When we let go of glibly assigning an oversimplified cause to human interactions, and look for *how* things happen, we find that reality is quite complex with numerous antecedent "causes."

The Immediate, Practical Cause

And even after this elaborate explanation of what caused Frank to hit Bill, we still haven't fully answered the question "What caused Bill to get angry?" In trying to understand my own behavior and that of other people, I find it helpful to look for the *immediate, practical cause* of all emotional reactions. It is more practical and empowering to see Bill's anger when he was hit by Frank as *immediately* caused by Bill's programming. Thus we conclude that Bill's anger is only secondarily caused by Frank, Frank's programming, or Frank's history of child abuse. Bill got angry because of his own programming that caused *him* to react with anger when he was hit by Frank.

To help Bill live a happier life, he would be more effective if he focused on the *immediate, practical cause of his anger*, which was *his own programming* rather than Frank's actions. Bill may be much more successful in changing his addictive demand into a preferential response than in trying to change Frank's behavior (which really depends on Frank more than on anything Bill may do). If Bill used preferential programming in responding to the situation, he would not have felt angry; instead, he might have felt compassion and inner peace. And he would have been wiser in dealing with Frank. Bill has the ultimate ability to change his programming and create serenity and happiness for himself, no matter what anyone else does or says.

By improving your precision in diagnosing cause and effect in human interactions, you can empower yourself to live a happier life. There are *severe limits* to how much you can control the world (antecedent conditions), which activates your various demanding programs that trigger your fear, frustration, anger, irritation, resentment, hatred, jealousy, anxiety—all of which adds up to your unhappiness. There is *no limit* to your ability to modify your own programming if you are determined to do so. It will take time and patience to deal with the big ones. It will really happen when you want to create your own happiness more than you want to try to control everything that happens around you.

Giving Yourself the Gift of Growth

Everything that exists is in a process of change. Some things change rapidly, like the weather. Other things change slowly, like the wrinkles on your face. To feel at home in this world, you must avoid being addicted to the status quo.

Each day of your life may be regarded as a school for personal growth. All your addictive programming, such as demands about sex, money, pride, or prestige, will probably offer you a chance for growth. Your subconscious core beliefs, or "injured inner child" scars on your mind, make you vulnerable to creating the experiences of separateness and alienation.

You can regard your addictive demands and your inner child dysfunctions as opposite sides of the same coin. The addictive demands are more in the spotlight of your awareness; the injured child programmings are usually hidden below your awareness in your subconscious mind.

Any inner child injuries that are not healed will sooner or later surface in your behavior as addictive demands. Since the roots of these demands lie in the vast subconscious, your study in this area can really pay off in increasing your happiness.*

Your day-to-day life experiences will give you all the practice you need for your personal growth—if you use them. Remember that the difference between heaven and earth is not so much a matter of *altitude*—as it is of *attitude*.

---

* Some of the popular books in this field are *Self-Parenting: The Complete Guide to Your Inner Conversations* by John K. Pollard, III (Generic Human Studies Publishing, 1987), *Facing Codependence: What It Is, Where It Comes From, How It Sabotages Our Lives* by Pia Mellody (Harper and Row, 1987), *Breaking Free: A Recovery Workbook for Facing Codependence* by Pia Mellody and Andrea Wells Miller (Harper & Row, 1989), *Codependent No More: How to Stop Controlling Others and Start Caring for Yourself* by Melody Beattie (Harper and Row, 1987), and *Choicemaking: For Co-Dependents, Adult Children and Spirituality Seekers* by Sharon Wegscheider-Cruse (Health Communications, Inc., 1985).

4

Be Aware That Falling in Love Is Not a Basis for Commitment.

"Falling in love is not a basis for commitment? That's crazy," you may say to yourself. I must admit that it does sound crazy—especially coming from the founder of a Science of Happiness, which includes "Living Love." But perhaps it's crazy wisdom.

The problem is that most of us operate from a great deficiency of love. We often didn't experience enough love in our childhood, and our hearts hunger for this satisfying feeling. We are on the lookout for people who seem to accept and love us. And when we find a person who appears to feel some love for us, it's a tremendous event. We believe that love is so scarce we have to do something about it. Cage it. Tie it up. Don't let it get away! Marry it!

As we develop skill in loving everyone unconditionally, including ourselves, we begin to create lives that are not deficient in love. We increasingly create and live in a warm world of appreciation, emotional acceptance, heart-to-heart feelings, and unconditional love with more and more people.

As we reach past our separate-self demands, we learn to emotionally accept people as they are. Our hearts feel the preciousness of each person. By working on our addictive models of how people "should" be, we begin to experience an ever widening compassionate acceptance and love for each human being as they are right now—with all their foibles and failings. The people around us notice the way we are increasingly radiating unconditional love for them even when we don't like what they do or say. They like being with someone who is *living love*. It's like finding an oasis in the desert.

As I learned to love unconditionally, I began to live in a world of love. I've now learned to operate my mind and heart so that I can feel love and acceptance toward everybody—most of the time. And I work on my programming quickly if my ego hits me with a demand that throws me out of my unified-self feelings.

Thus I cannot use love as a basis for involvement in an intimate relationship because *love becomes my general experience of everybody*. I no longer live in a vacuum in which I am blown around by every breath of lovely fresh air.

So if you are effectively working on yourself to love everyone unconditionally, you cannot use love as a basis for commitment. You'll increasingly be loving everybody—and you can't be intimately involved in a partnership with everyone you love.

How Do We Choose?

If we don't use love as a basis for commitment, what do we use? There are over five billion people on earth. It's important to carefully select a partner with whom you can create the higher levels of communication, caring, and commitment. How do we go about choosing a life partner?

Three criteria have worked for me. You may wish to ask yourself these questions:

1. **Do you like just *being* with her or him?** You may be so busy entertaining yourselves *doing* things together that neither of you knows if you just like *being* with each other. Try going on a camping trip for a week with no one else around.

Do you really enjoy being near each other? Continuously? Do you like them as a human *being*— or as a human *doing?*

2. **Are you willing to live with the other person's programming (addictive, "injured child," and otherwise), and is that person willing to live with yours?** Emotional honesty during dating lets a prospective partner really get to experience your programming as much as possible, and *vice versa.* The game is not just to get into a committed relationship—it's to live happily ever after.*

   Can your prospective partner emotionally accept your moods and attitudes? Does this person explode or sulk or cower when you are irritated or upset? Are you addicted if they respond this way? Can you handle it if both of you start bouncing off each other's demands? Can you usually feel compassion instead of threat if they blow up?

   In my second marriage, which ended in divorce, I planned on my partner's changing in ways I wanted after we were married. It didn't work. I learned that I shouldn't choose a mate the way I might get a house—not responding to things as they are but as they'd be when I got them remodeled!

3. **Do you like to do many things together?** Or do your egos compete or clash as you try to cooperate? Are your interests, goals, values, tastes,

---

* I'm not using the word "game" in a negative sense as Eric Berne in *Games People Play* used it to point to a dishonest ploy for misleading someone. I'm using "game" in its basic meaning as in "a game of cards." From this point of view, we create the experience of life as a fun game to be played rather than a heavy load of problems to be solved.

and philosophies sufficiently similar so that you enjoy creating the adventure of life together?

When Penny and I do things together, we often feel like two kids playing. A heart love automatically turns on that enlivens and enriches whatever we're doing. After 11 years of being together, we can experience shopping, traveling, watching a movie, or working on a book together as a romantic adventure. As the background scenery on the stage of our lives continually changes, we just keep on playing out our love script.

Here are some suggestions from one of our workshops:

You wouldn't choose to be involved with every person. You can't. So how do you make your choice? You base it on whose addictions you're willing to make OK. Now if you say, "I can make everybody's addictions OK," then it gets down to whom do you want to play with? Who plays the same games in a similar enough way that you enjoy playing with them?

But it's never "romantic love," which just sets up a booby trap. We're in trouble when we tell ourselves that love is special—unique. Then we've got to hang on. "I can't let this person go because this is the only person I'm able to love." Or in terms of what we're discussing, "I'm hanging on because this is the only person I've met whose programming reflects my programming enough so that I can get in touch with the parts of me that I love." That's what you're saying.

It's a self-fulfilling prophecy because that's the person you set up to share with on that level. We all have parts of each other within ourselves. Our programming is so similar. And our inner work means creating that "safe space" with more and more people—"safe" because we can handle our addictions when they come up. Which is what you're going to start doing. And as you start doing it, you start seeing the potential for relationships that you have in your life. There are many people that I could choose to be married to and enjoy it thoroughly. Just totally enjoy it! Then it just gets down to the fine sifting.

Putting it another way, if a loving person were to use *only* love as a basis for choosing a partner, it would be like using the existence of a steering wheel for deciding which car to buy. Since all cars have steering wheels, we need other criteria for deciding.

When you're doing a good job of handling your demands and loving unconditionally, your life will be filled with love! Then you can choose a partner who likes to play the same life games together—to celebrate life together. Thus love no longer serves as a definitive guideline for selecting a partner. You are learning to love everyone unconditionally—including yourself.

5

*Can You Share
Life Together
in a Way
That Contributes
to Your Mutual
Well-Being?*

Two people living together may make many contributions to each other's well-being. These can range from coordinating household activities to empathetically listening to each other's feelings and thoughts and supporting each other's interests and dreams.

Your unified-self can help you feel that your relationship as a couple is a priceless treasure in your life. The unconditional love in your heart will inspire you to give more and more to your beloved. This giving will not come from fear or weakness, or from a desire to get something from your partner. It will instead be an overflowing of the cornucopia of love in your heart. Your heart will want your partner to have the most wonderful life possible in your relationship together.

You can learn to regard each opportunity to love and serve your beloved as a gift your life is giving you. You use your love and creativity to discover ways that are best for you—and your relationship. Your partner's delight brings you pleasure.

The willpower contest of "me vs. them" becomes less frequent. Your trust in the power of unconditional love can increase year by year as you use the challenging sparks of your disagreements to practice letting go of your demands—and growing into your unified-self.

As the unified-self energy evolves, you will find many ways to express the overflowing love in your heart—both verbally and nonverbally. Penny and I spontaneously say "I love you" many times each day. We like to touch each other and we usually sit in a way that allows contact. I feel my life is enhanced as I continuously bathe in love for my beloved Penny.

Growing Beyond Your Separate-Self

There are a number of things I have learned in growing beyond the separate-self to the unified-self with a partner. Here are some that have helped me contribute to our mutual well-being:

Hiding our feelings and thoughts from our partner perpetuates our separate-self. Many people try to keep a phony front and honeyed-over peace in their relationship by carefully avoiding saying or doing things that trigger their partner's fear, frustration, or anger. Although we always wish to act gently, if we develop the habit of "walking on eggs" so as not to ever trigger our partner's separate-self programming, we may not be communicating our own living truth. And pretending to be where we aren't does not move us toward intimacy in a relationship.

I can contribute to our mutual well-being by appreciating and enjoying the "enoughness" in our relationship. In a partnership (as well as in life) we often tend to focus on what we don't have—and unconsciously take for granted the abundance we do have. We open our hearts to happiness by not demanding or stewing over what we don't have.

In the past, my separate-self created the illusion that if I constantly pointed out the deficiencies of my partner, she would be motivated to give me more of what I wanted. I found this wasn't effective. I often got more of what I didn't want!

If you catch your ego trying to bribe, coerce, or shame your partner into giving you what you want, don't put yourself down. These "right-wrong" games of the separate-self are only a stage of growth. Be gentle and compassionate with yourself. With awareness, you can grow beyond these separate-self ego habits.

The Five Freedoms

Dr. Virginia Satir formulated a psychological bill of rights. She calls these the "five freedoms":

- The freedom to see and hear what is here and now, rather than what was, will be or should be—and to be able to share it.
- The freedom to think what one thinks, rather than what one should think—and to be able to share it.
- The freedom to feel what one feels, rather than what one should feel—and to be able to share it.
- The freedom to want and to choose what one wants, rather than what one should want—and to be able to share it.
- And the freedom to imagine one's own self-actualization, rather than playing a rigid role or always playing it safe—and to be able to share it.

You can contribute to your mutual well-being by giving these five freedoms to yourself and your partner. In my brief marriage with Bonita, I made myself upset when she felt angry toward me. I now realize that my separate-self ego was not giving Bonita the freedom to feel what she was feeling. I thought her anger meant something about me. I now know it was only her own programming that made her feel angry. I used to feel I should defend myself. I know now that it's OK for my partner to feel upset, critical, or whatever. And I've learned that my partner can get

45

herself through these unpleasant emotions much quicker if I allow her the five freedoms and don't make her wrong for having them. And giving her these freedoms does not necessarily mean I agree with her.

As day by day you gradually increase your skill in offering yourself and your partner these five freedoms, you will enable the power of unconditional love to carry your life into a new dimension of enjoyment. And you will increasingly experience yourself as a *creative cause* in your life! You will no longer feel hopeless and helpless as a *victim* of circumstances beyond your control. As you open yourself to the unifying energy of unconditional love, your life can be miraculously transformed into heights of insight, joy, and happiness that you never thought possible.

Trusting the Power of Unconditional Love

To demand things of your partner is human; to let go of separating demands is divine. The love in your heart will help you accept that your partner can only use the programming they now have. And if real change (instead of coerced, surface, phony change) is to take place, your unconditional love provides a reinforcing environment for your partner's growth.

The best way to help your partner experience greater love is for *you* to create in yourself an experience of greater love for him or her. And I mean do it *first.* And continuously. And keep doing it whether or not you get the "results" you desire. To really get results, you must strip your love of all its conditionality. For the power of love does not work best when you expect to get something back.

Many years ago, I decided to work on making it OK not to get anything from my partner that she could

46

not give me with love in her heart. I wanted to trust that the love in her heart would usually enable her to want to give me what I desired. And when it didn't, I told myself that my insisting on something could only create separateness.

As love deepens, partners can give more and more to each other. Love bridges over what cannot be given without resentment. Trusting the power of love to help me get what's freely gettable without the penalty of separateness has worked for me. I *try* to love and serve my partner by letting go of any demand for what she can't give me with good feelings. Sometimes I can let go; sometimes I can't. And I feel that my partner gives me many times more than I need to be happy in our marriage.

> *When you love someone, you are perceptive of your beloved's relationship to their own life—and not exclusively concerned with their relationship to your life.*

You love a person because they're there—not because they need, merit, or deserve your love. After reading this sentence, someone wrote me, "Does this mean you should love *all* people simply because they are human beings?" I'm not saying you "should" love all people. Love doesn't work as a "should." I'm saying that *if* you want to experience more happiness, loving is *how* you do it. The main reason I'm advocating that we unconditionally love all people is that it is the very best way I have found to feel good. And we humans basically want to feel happy and fulfilled.

When you learn to radiate your love simply because it is the best way to be good to yourself, this pure love will automatically produce the most that is attainable in a relationship between two people. So tell your ego to relax and make it OK not to get everything it wants in a relationship. Because that's the way life is: *You win some and you lose some.*

What Is Your Level of Commitment?

Research by Dr. Brent Barlow of Brigham Young University indicates that communication, caring, and commitment are the foundation of an enjoyable relationship: *Communication*, both verbal and non-verbal, enables *caring* to develop and be maintained. As communication and caring develop, a lifetime *commitment* on deeper and deeper levels may begin to unfold.

> *You don't have to stay stuck forever in a marriage that just doesn't work out. However, it takes a lot of communication, caring, and commitment to make any marriage work.*

As you consider going into a relationship, *look deeply into your heart and mind to discover your level of commitment to the other person's well-being.* In my second marriage I had a deep level of communication and caring. (I had taken enough psychology courses to understand the importance of coming out of hiding.) I deeply cared for Bonita. Although I didn't comprehend it at the time, my level of commitment was shaky.

I'd previously been in an 18-year marriage. I told myself that if my next marriage didn't work out with a lot of harmony in the first year, I'd just wash it down the drain and start again. And with my addiction that she not be occasionally moody and possessive, I did just that. Today using the guidelines in this book, I could easily handle these demands and transform them into preferences before they chipped away at my love.

What Are Your Limits?

Amy loves to sew for Henry. She makes him several shirts every Christmas and for all his birthdays. Henry doesn't like any of them. They are not the colors or style he would choose. Yet he is afraid he will hurt her feelings if he tells her so. Therefore, he never lets her know how he actually feels about them. He reluctantly wears them to please her although he feels conspicuous and silly. His friends don't help matters any with teasing comments like "Wearing another one of your wife's shirts, eh?" He responds to the situation by "losing" as many of them as he can without being too obvious. But she keeps making more.

No matter how much Henry wants to appreciate Amy's sewing for him, he still feels embarrassed and resentful. Henry is giving a "gift" to Amy that he can't afford to give. He is allowing her to think she is making him wonderful shirts that he likes. It would be more effective for him—and a truer gift to Amy—if he would gently face the issue with her, suggest that she make shirts for the homeless as a possible solution, and risk her reaction—which couldn't be any worse for him than what he is already experiencing.

What are you willing to "be with" from day to day? There are some "gifts" you cannot afford to give if you later resent giving them. Be realistic—it's kindest over a period of time.

Learn as much as you can about your partner's programming before entering into a commitment. I would not go into a relationship with a person who challenged my habits of mind so strongly that I would have to constantly be working on myself to stay centered. I try to at least set up my relationship for fun. And then I work on what life gives me—which will be plenty! And I must resist my ego if it tempts me with the illusion that a good partner is one who doesn't disagree with me. The goal is to create a relationship that can deal constructively with disagreements.

From time to time, your partner may want things on which you do not want to spend time, energy, or money. What are your limits? And make it OK to have them. Everyone has them—and they expand further and further as you grow in unconditional love.

Time, space, and energy are gifts from the universe. But your separate-self may make you feel that it is "your time," "your space," and "your energy." Your ego often will not permit you to give these gifts without developing a feeling of resentment or a bookkeeping approach: "I've done this for you, so now you owe me something." While it is lovely to give, you can create the feeling of separateness if your ego keeps pointing out what you have given.

The consistent winners in the love game learn to serve their partner without the self-consciousness that they—as separate individuals—are doing it. They have a unified-self feeling that they're helping US—not just helping someone else. It's a feeling of one hand washing the other.

Your Mutual Well-Being

So, in choosing a partner, you might ask yourself to what degree you can contribute to the well-being of your partner on their terms. This means asking your partner what they like and want. It means looking deeply into your heart and mind to find to what extent you can appreciate your relationship as an opportunity to love and serve your beloved.

Through your unified-self, you show your partner over and over that you'll be there for them. You listen to them and talk about what is meaningful to each of you. You keep fun and romance alive in your own heart so you can share them with your beloved.

The great power of unconditional love as unfolded by your unified-self can help you enrich both of your lives. And we experience the truth of St. Francis of Assisi, "It is in giving that we receive."

6

Honor Your Differences.

Differences between relationship partners are as certain as the sun's rising tomorrow. When a French Deputy said that there are few differences between men and women today, someone in the audience shouted out, "Vive la différence!"—long live the difference!

Differences that we like are no problem. Differences we don't like give us practice in loving unconditionally. When we honor our differences, we make the most of the best and the least of the worst.

My mind can come up with a long list of "should's" that no human being or relationship could possibly meet. I don't want my ideals of perfection to ruin my relationship as it did in the past. I try to use them the way a lighthouse guides a ship; I don't wreck my relationship trying to get to the lighthouse. Thurman Arnold, a noted U.S. Assistant Attorney General, said that the greatest killer of ideals is one who cannot adapt them to the practical realities of one's life.

The Great Adventure of Life

I like the lift I get by viewing my relationship as a way of cooperating in the great adventure of life. This perspective sets up an energy of fun and enjoyment. It suggests flowing through life—instead of plowing through it.

Using this as a guide, I hunted for someone who liked to participate in activities I enjoyed. It also reminded me to look at whether I'd feel good cooperating in the things she liked to do.

Of course, I don't expect 100 percent agreement—life isn't like that. I'm thankful if my partner likes to cooperate with me in three-fourths of the things I like to do. Penny and I seem to have a high batting average. We both like being together snuggling while we watch TV movies she's recorded, getting away in a motor home, taking care of our bodies through exercise and healthy eating (including a regimen of vitamin and mineral supplements), listening to classical music, occasionally speaking to groups, doing things that give us the feeling we're making meaningful contributions in the world, plus many, many other ways we create our life together.

Some of our differences include: She likes chatting in bed at night and would rather sleep a little longer in the morning; I usually fall asleep when my head hits the pillow and I like to spring up and greet the new day around six in the morning. I like our living quarters to be warm during the day and to have cool fresh air at night; Penny's the reverse. I like cruising on the water; she gets queasy when the ship rolls. She enjoys hiking and bicycling; I can't do these things. I like movies with sexual situations; she has limits. She likes Danny Kaye movies; I've been known to fall asleep during them. I like to watch football on TV; Penny finds other things to do. She'd like to have a baby; I've had children and now I want other commitments.

Many of our differences enrich life for both of us. She's family-oriented and keeps track of birthdays and deepens bonds across the miles; I'm global family-oriented and keep track of international relations and how to bring permanent peace to our planet.

We love producing books as a team, and we turn out a better job together than either of us could do alone. We have written several books together. Her thoroughness for detail and astute editing skills make them more reader friendly. With our distinctive and diverse skills, we offer balance to each other.

Expecting Differences

To have contrasting leanings and inclinations is typical of most men and women. Some differences may go back to early childhood. One research project involving four-year-old boys and girls found that all the sounds made by little girls were related to words. The girls spent half their time talking to each other and half their time talking to themselves. They found that only sixty percent of the sounds made by little boys related to actual words. Forty percent were action sounds, such as KA-BOOM! RUMM! BZZZ. BAMM!

This early difference in the use of language continues in modified form as we grow older. It has been found that in about four out of five homes, women tend to use language that relates to the feelings of the heart, and men lean more toward the project-oriented, factual, and logical language of the head. Although there are many individual exceptions, generalizations can sometimes be useful in giving us a broader perspective of ourselves.

Penny tends to be more people-oriented; I tend to be more project-oriented. Like a bulldozer, in the past I have sometimes put projects ahead of people. Although I care how people feel, I can more easily override this concern to effectively complete an undertaking on time. While Penny also likes to get the job done, she can more easily override the time schedule to check out people's feelings and respond to their concerns and interests. When Penny and I honor and communicate about our differences, we both benefit—and we usually get a project completed on time in a way that feels as good as possible to everyone.

Honoring Our Differences

When partners honor their differences, they tend to build their effectiveness as a couple—and cancel out deficiencies as individuals. One partner may be a saver who squirrels away money for a rainy day; the other may like to use money for heightening the here-and-now enjoyment of life. With skillful communication, caring, and commitment, these different points of view may help partners find a more balanced wisdom in daily life.

When we revere the ways in which we differ from our partner, we can feel respect mingled with love and devotion. Each partner has things they can learn from the other as the separate-self egos let go of trying to prove who's "right" and who's "wrong." And then we can enlarge our appreciation of the preciousness and value that each of us contributes. In this way, the potential of our partnership is enhanced by the diversity of our differences.

7

Don't Expect the Relationship to Make You Happy.

The opportunity to live in physical, emotional, intellectual, and spiritual intimacy with another human being is one of life's greatest gifts. You can damage and bruise this gift by your expectations and demands that the relationship make you happy. Sorry, but no one's going to make you happy.

The number and strength of your dysfunctional inner child programs and addictive demands are the crucial factors in creating your personal experience of happiness. You don't suddenly *find* happiness in a relationship; you *take* happiness into your relationship.

Here are ingredients for creating more and more intimacy in your marriage:

- You are in touch with your emotions and can deal with your addictive demands and "injured child" programming.
- You can communicate your thoughts, feelings, and desires, and listen to your partner's.
- You genuinely appreciate and love yourself.
- You deeply love and care for your partner.
- You are committed to making your relationship work.

In the normal course of living together, your relationship will put you in touch with your addictive demands and unfinished inner child resentments. But since you can use these experiences for your growth, "problems" in your relationship can help you make the rest of your life more enjoyable—IF. . . . The big "if" is your determination to skillfully use your life situations for your own growth.

> *Everyone and everything become your teachers. Problems are a gift your life offers you to help you grow.*

You'll make yourself unhappy if you burden your relationship with the expectation of eliminating what you don't like about your life—or of giving you everything you do want. If, for example, your demanding programming insists on having sex almost every day, your partner may resent your demands. The only thing you can dependably expect from your relationship is the opportunity to use your life situations for your growth. Then you will find that you always have "enough" in your life.

You Can Still Disagree

Remember, emotionally accepting does not mean that you don't try to change something. It just means that you don't waste your energy in anger, irritation, resentment, fear, or frustration. Your personal growth helps you to emotionally accept what you can't change. And then you intelligently focus your energy onto making whatever changes are possible without setting up new problems in your life.

Let's see how this can work. Fran was married to Joe, who was in graduate school. She typed his term papers for him. Whenever she completed an essay for him, he invariably pointed out to her any typing or spelling errors she had made. That would have been OK with her. However, he pointed them out in a loud, sarcastic, and demeaning way. Fran often shared with him how she felt when he criticized her so harshly.

However, Joe's programming made him continue to loudly blame her whenever she made a mistake.

Fran had a challenge. She wanted to keep the love in her heart for Joe, so she chose to learn to emotionally accept his criticism. From then on whenever he loudly berated her, she calmly thanked him for making her aware of the mistake, told him she preferred that he communicate to her in a less blaming manner, and returned to what she was doing. Each time she practiced this, she felt calmer and more centered. She *preferred* that Joe talk to her in a more loving way—and she *accepted* that he might never change. Most of all, she realized that no matter what Joe said or did, he was not the cause of her happiness—or unhappiness. Fran in this situation realized that she did not have to feel like a victim of Joe's separate-self behavior. She could instead be the creative cause of her experience.

What Causes Happiness and Unhappiness?

To understand why your relationship will not make you happy, let's delve more deeply into the immediate, practical cause of unhappiness in an adult human life. You'll recall the First Wisdom Principle we discussed in Chapter 3: My addictive demands trigger my separating emotions, which create my unhappiness. Preferences never do.

As you look closely at your life situations, you will notice that your addictive, emotion-backed demands are the immediate, practical cause of unhappiness. And your preferences promote your happiness.

The life situation is not as important as your programming in creating your moment-to-moment happiness. This diagram shows how Fran's internal emotional experience of Joe is created by her addictive or preferential programming—not by the life event:

HOW DEMANDS AND PREFERENCES WORK

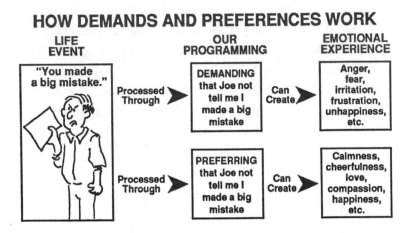

LIFE EVENT	OUR PROGRAMMING		EMOTIONAL EXPERIENCE
"You made a big mistake."	DEMANDING that Joe not tell me I made a big mistake	Can Create	Anger, fear, irritation, frustration, unhappiness, etc.
	PREFERRING that Joe not tell me I made a big mistake	Can Create	Calmness, cheerfulness, love, compassion, happiness, etc.

As we've discussed, our demands are emotion-backed habits of mind (programs) that automatically trigger our own anger, irritation, fear, resentment, boredom, grief, etc., when life is not giving us what we want. For example, if I'm addicted to your not criticizing me, and you say something critical, I automatically become angry. Did I become angry because you criticized me? No! I got angry because *my programming demanded* that you not criticize me. *My demand is the direct cause of my anger; my anger is the effect (or symptom) of my demand.*

None of us is responsible for all the things that happen to us. But as adults we are responsible for how we react when they do happen.

Suppose I lose $30 from my pocket. If I demand (instead of prefer) to hold onto my money, I will automatically create a separating emotion, such as worry or irritation. If I am addicted to your picking up your clothes, like a good addictive robot I will make myself create the experience of irritation if you leave your clothes on the floor. If I'm addicted to your being on time, I'll upset myself if you're late. My addictive demands are like land mines waiting for me to step on!

Penalties We Pay for Addictive Demands

It's obvious that when I don't get my demand satisfied, I make myself unhappy. However, even when I do get my demand satisfied, I may increase my demands or I may worry about losing whatever it was that I got. So getting what I want may actually add to the load of addictions I'm carrying around. Our separate-self egos don't often let us relax and enjoy what we have. They drive us to want more and more.

Addictions make us reject situations in our lives and automatically trigger unpleasant emotions. When we continually produce alienating emotions, we make ourselves unhappy. Our addictive programming creates our illusory, distorted experience with:

- Regrets and upsetting memories of the past.
- Worries for the future.
- Tension in our bodies.
- A narrow view of current life events.
- Unpleasant emotional reactions, such as anger, fear, frustration, shame, guilt, jealousy, hatred, irritation, and resentment.
- Plus all the right-wrong rationalizing that our minds are so good at.

63

Addictive demands are thus the enemies of our happiness. They can keep us trapped in anxiety and confusion. They can affect our bodies and create tension, uneasiness, sleeplessness, and often pain and illness. Our demanding programming can stimulate our minds to be judgmental, critical, and blaming of ourselves and others. It will dominate our consciousness and limit our skill in loving unconditionally.

When we look closely at our addictive demands, we often discover there is a recurrent, dysfunctional pattern to them. These addictions have not only harmed us in the past, they also threaten our future if not healed.

Demands Load Us With Stress

Let's take a closer look at the life-killing consequences of addictions. Addictions hamper our insight into what is happening in our lives. They make us unable to appreciate the beauty that is here and now, and they keep us trapped in a distorted understanding of life events. Our demands waste our energy in bodily tensions and emotional drains. They make us worried, anxious, afraid, disappointed, frustrated, bored, impatient, angry, disdainful, hateful. As a wise man put it, "To set up what you like against what you dislike is the disease of the mind."

When we are stuck in addictively demanding, we keep perpetuating certain patterns or problems in our lives that discourage people from wanting to be with us. Demands also make us inflexible and block our creativity. They create the illusory experience that life is an endless series of conflicts. They make mountains out of molehills.

Our demanding programming limits our alternatives and choices. It keeps us trapped in "tunnel vision," in which we tend to respond mechanically and recognize few options. We are often unable to even enjoy what we have because we are addictively clinging to it for fear of losing it.

Addictive demands programmed in our minds make us emotionally or intellectually reject ourselves and others. Thus they keep us from loving ourselves and others. They make us miss the fun of creating a happier life.

Addictions limit our ability to make changes in our lives. And even when we do make a change, it's often at the price of being bruised from trying to forcefully control people or situations. What's more, addictions often create the experience that we still don't have "enough." The Greek philosopher Epicurus warned us, "Do not spoil what you have by desiring what you have not."

Having told all the mischief addictions cause, it's timely to now say that addictions are not good or bad—or right or wrong. They aren't like sin! And you can still trade them in for preferences. It's OK to have addictive demands!

‖ Don't demand to have no demands.

It's normal to have addictive demands. It's also normal to be unhappy. Who wants to be normal in these ways?

Yet if addictions do so much to screw up our lives, why do we hold on to them? Why don't we drop them like hot potatoes? That's an important question. The answer lies in an illusion: we think we get "payoffs" by holding on to our demands.

"Payoffs" Keep Us Stuck in Our Demands

Our egos often hold on to our demanding programming because we are willing to settle for certain payoffs—even though the overall effect of the addiction is that of creating separateness and unhappiness in our lives. And so we continually postpone happiness. Some of the payoffs that keep us stuck in our addictive programs are:

- "I get to be right and make the other person wrong."
- "I get to feel superior."
- "I'll prove it's unfair or untrue."
- "It feels safe and familiar to hold on to old programming, and scary to let it go."
- "My demand that I be different will force me to change my behavior."
- "I get sympathy from other people who have the same addiction."
- "I feel really alive when I get angry. I like my adrenaline rush."
- "If I get angry enough, they may do what I want."
- "They'll make it up to me because they'll see how upset I am, and they'll feel shamed or guilty."
- "If I'm upset, I'll have an excuse for poor performance."

Suppose Fred has an addictive demand that his wife, Justine, not talk on the phone to her friends while they are eating dinner. He wants dinner time to be a quality time for just the two of them. He creates resentment, anger, and righteous indignation whenever one of her friends calls and she spends the rest of the meal chatting. Fred holds on to his demand because he has a payoff: he's "right" and she's "wrong."

He has a perfect right to want to spend time alone with Justine. And she's obviously wrong for not honoring their special private time together. He

66

sulks, makes noise by clanking the silverware, and glares at her indignantly. When she finally does get off the phone, Fred gives her a verbal jab with, "You've ruined another evening together. You are insensitive and a bore!" He then stomps off to the living room with the evening paper.

What could happen if Fred becomes aware that his payoff isn't working? He knows his payoff (being "right") is getting him nowhere with his demand that Justine not talk on the phone during dinner. He realizes that the love they share and true harmony between them is more important than his demand. The next time Justine is on the phone, Fred covers her plate with aluminum foil to keep it warm and continues to calmly eat his meal. He internally reminds himself that he can let go of the "payoff" of righteousness. He still prefers that Justine not talk on the phone. When Justine gets off the phone, Fred says, "I prefer that we have meal times as private time together." If Justine continues to allow mealtime interruptions, he realizes that he can look for creative ways that will let them both get their underlying interests met, and he can accept that it is not happening—for now. He has kept the love in his heart.*

Usually the payoffs we think we're getting never really happen. When we look at the lost happiness, lost joy, lost intimacy, and lost love, we begin to see that we are paying heavily for our addictive demands. We recognize that these payoffs are a very poor substitute for the aliveness and love we enjoy when we use preferential filters.

* Some helpful techniques are presented in *Getting Together: Building a Relationship That Gets to Yes* by Roger Fisher and Scott Brown (Houghton Mifflin Company, 1988).

The Pleasure of Preferences

A preference is the oil that takes the friction out of life. When we transform our addictions to preferences, we can ride the waves and thoroughly enjoy our lives.

Preferences enable us to focus on creatively finding more effective choices. They help us develop "the serenity to accept the things I cannot change, the courage to change the things I can, and the wisdom to know the difference." Through preferences we can appreciate our lives—instead of continually postponing happiness until things change in the future. Some things may never change!

Preferences help us avoid feeling like we're living on the edge of a cliff. With preferential programming, we can calmly respond to circumstances with spontaneity, creativity, and insight.

Preferences help us handle the ups and downs of our lives—instead of continually knocking our heads against a brick wall. They help us emotionally accept the "impossible," do without the "indispensable," and skillfully handle the "intolerable."

Preferences let us view the melodrama of our lives from a larger perspective. They allow us to notice many choices and to be open to a wide variety of options and possibilities that may help us get what we prefer.

I've often been amazed at how anger and hatred corrode our happiness. It was a wise person who wrote, "Hatred does a great deal more damage to the vessel in which it is stored than the object on which it is poured."

You've heard the old adage "When angry, count to ten." I'd like to revise it: "When angry, count to ten—*then* work on reprogramming your addictive demand into a preference." When we do this our anger disappears because what made us angry—our demand—has disappeared. The next time a similar situation arises, the addictive program may be weaker—or gone. And the creative parts of our mind will access new ways to preferentially respond to a challenge.

Accelerating Your Growth

"Real happiness," wrote educator William Lyon Phelps, "is not dependent on external things. The pond is fed from within. The kind of happiness that stays with you is the happiness that springs from inward thoughts and emotions. . . ."

Skill in applying the guidelines in this book can help you develop the happiness that comes from inward thoughts and emotions. Three factors are essential in giving yourself this skill:

1. A good *understanding* that enables you to identify your demands in daily life. It will be helpful to reread this chapter several times. But knowledge alone won't work.

2. A *determination* to give yourself this skill.

3. A lot of *practice* doing it. Throughout this book you can get insights on how to practice. You may create your own inner techniques to escape from the agony of addictive demands. Chapter 10 has additional suggestions.

Your mind is not set in concrete. You are not your programming. You are a precious essence of humanity. Your patience and willingness to work on your personal growth can enable you to increase your enjoyment of your life. And as you experience more enjoyment, you strengthen your commitment to use every situation for your own personal growth.

In Summary

When you let go of the expectation that a relationship will make you happy or wipe out everything you don't like about your life, you improve your opportunity for happiness. You can begin to appreciate a relationship for the things it gives you. The greatest richness initially is that you can absolutely count on a relationship to give you lots of opportunities for personal growth! Whether or not you use them is up to you.

> *The key to living a happy life lies in turning down your addictive demands and turning up your love.*

We've discovered that it is unrealistic to expect our relationship to make us happy. No person or thing can make us happy. *It's up to us to make ourselves happy.* All our relationship can do is to furnish a cast of characters for our melodrama. It's up to us whether we act out a preferential adventure or an addictively demanding tragedy.

We've now examined seven guidelines for going into a relationship. Now we're ready for the next step—seven guidelines for creating a delightful relationship with the partner we've chosen.

70

PART II

Seven Guidelines for Creating a Delightful Relationship

8

*Communicate
Deeper and Deeper
Levels of Honesty.*

Usually, honesty simply means that we are no longer lying to our partner. By deeper honesty we mean sharing with our partner the thoughts and actions our separate-self ego wants to hide.

Most of us have discovered that lying can create a lot of problems. When you tell a lie, you must always remember exactly what lie you told and who you told it to—or you'll trip up later. It's embarrassing when the lie is discovered. Sooner or later you will be caught, and then trust is undermined. There is no way you can get the most from your relationship if trust is lacking. Trust is built by full communication.

The desire to conceal is created by your addictions, and thus it furnishes a clue to the next steps in your inner work. To build the most loving and joyful experience in living with your beloved, you may wish to stop doing things you are not willing to share. *It's OK to think anything—but be willing to share it.*

Deeper Honesty

One of your greatest challenges as a human being lies in the development of a deeper and deeper level of honesty. This means totally opening yourself—no secrets! Your separate-self ego may try to intimidate you by whispering, "It's too embarrassing, too humiliating, too risky to be honest about." If you are seduced by this separate-self voice, you become enmeshed in a web of concealment.

John Bradshaw tells us, "We are as sick as our secrets." If you're not deeply honest and open, your partner is living with your "act"—not you. Your intimate relationship needs living truth as much as your lungs need pure air.

Deeper honesty requires you to trust that you are naturally lovable when you are being yourself. If you are unable to share your inner thoughts, it means you think you have to conceal a part of you from your beloved. Believing you have to hide your thoughts and feelings chips away at intimacy and togetherness—and you psychologically experience your partner as "her" or "him"—not "us." In the deeper levels of your mind, you create "me *vs.* my partner"—not "me *and* my partner." This can make you cast your partner as an adversary.

Connie has an eating disorder. She often overeats until she is nearly bursting, and then vomits to relieve the tension and pain in her stomach. She has been married to Rick for three years and has never shared her bulimia problem with him. A few of her friends know about it, and yet she can't bring herself to tell her husband. It stemmed from a casual remark he had made very early in their relationship that he was so happy to be with a "normal" person who didn't have hang-ups.

Because she wants him to think she is "normal," she has carried out an intricate scheme of deception. She eats in the middle of the night when he is asleep. She makes a midnight trip to the neighbor's garbage can to get rid of telltale food wrappers. Most of all she is terrified that Rick will find out and leave her. It is on her mind constantly. She can't spend any time with him without being obsessed with the thought that he will discover her "ugly" secret, or that he already knows about it and is waiting to lay it on her. Connie's demand that Rick not find out has caused her to encase herself in a world of illusion and suffering that has enormously compounded her problems. It has put a curtain of deceit around her relationship. A creeping separateness has set in.

When you aren't emotionally open with your partner, you're not trusting and loving yourself enough to be honest about your feelings. Yet your life is trying to tell you over and over again that separateness and hiding are not the way to get the deepest satisfaction from your relationship. "Telling the truth at any cost," Bradshaw advises, "means telling your feelings. That's the truth that'll make you free."

You Do It to Enrich Your Own Life

It takes a lot of work on yourself to develop a high level of honesty in your relationship. You may begin gradually and work up to the big ones. Or you may do it all at once. Good luck, however you do it!

Your ego may try to barter and say, "I'll expose myself if and when my partner is also deeply honest and open." This can block deeper honesty for an entire lifetime! Whether your partner is emotionally honest or not is their concern. You handicap yourself in creating your own experience of love if you do not choose to share your deeper inner thoughts and feelings with your beloved. And this includes greater honesty with yourself! Inner honesty is born of self-acceptance.

You learn to communicate deeper and deeper levels of honesty to improve your own experience of life. You're doing this to release *yourself* from a self-imposed jail of separateness. You're doing this to open up *your own* heart.

The purpose of deeper honesty is not to manipulate or "teach" your partner—although your ego may try to use your openness and frankness to pressure your partner to change. And when you are open and honest about your feelings, your partner may find it easier to be open—or perhaps even change!

Sometimes you hide your innermost feelings because you don't want to deal with what you will get in touch with when your partner reacts. Another ploy the separate-self ego uses to limit your honesty is an addictive fear of hurting the other person if you are totally open. "We can't afford to be so nice!" warns Ram Dass, a former Harvard psychology professor turned personal growth teacher.

> *The love that total honesty can create is worth whatever pain may be triggered when your honesty evokes your partner's embarrassment, fear, jealousy, resentment, or anger—or your own.*

You can feel compassion in your heart for all the vulnerable programming that everyone has. And at the same time accept that it exists, and realize that as long as it's there, it will probably be touched off from time to time.

Trusting Deeper Honesty

Give your partner the opportunity to take responsibility for creating their own experience—and to grow from it. Have confidence that sooner or later your partner can sort out their stuff. Remember that it is always your partner's expectations and demands that are the direct cause of their separating emotions—not the things you do or say. And, of course, what you do or say has consequences that you (and others) have to live with.

When you hide your real feelings, you're depriving your partner of the realities of life they need in order to deal with their own addictive demands. You can keep your relationship shallow if you have varying degrees of phoniness and avoidance.

And trying to hide your feelings really doesn't improve your relationship. Only a small percentage of your communication is through words, anyway. We all continuously communicate our real feelings on nonverbal levels through body language, tone of voice, gestures, and facial flickers. Your partner can intuitively sense that something is wrong—although they may not know exactly what it is.

When we overcome our hesitancy and learn to share our feelings and thoughts, we begin to break through our ego's pride and vanity programming. Our unified-self begins to replace our separate-self. And in the long run this is a very kind thing to do—kind both to ourselves and to our partner.

As a method for learning to communicate your living truth, you may find it helpful to repeat to yourself many times a day: "I open myself genuinely to all people by being willing to fully communicate my deepest feelings, since hiding in any degree keeps me stuck in my illusion of separateness from other people." (This is the Seventh Pathway, which appears on page 101.)

As your unconditional love unfolds for yourself and your partner, you will find it easier to communicate your deepest feelings. You will no longer let your ego get away with silently saying to your partner, "You stay out. These are my private feelings." Of course they're your private feelings. And the private separateness, private alienation, private loneliness, private hell, and private unhappiness are also your private possessions. Your unified-self does not need this privacy.

Suppressing, Expressing, Reprogramming

As children we may have been required by our parents to suppress our feelings. Most of us have cleanup work to do in this area. Freud's studies of the pernicious effects of repression and suppression launched an awareness of how crucial it is to express our feelings.

If we don't do something with the emotional energy that our bodies produce in response to the stresses of fear, frustration, or anger, we pay a heavy price. It's like sweeping the dirt under a rug; suppression makes things lumpy. It keeps us from loving ourselves and others. The feelings we hide can lead to headaches, high blood pressure and anxiety—and destroy the joy of living.

If you can't feel it, you can't heal it. So we've been encouraged to *express* our feelings rather than *suppress* them. It's a lot better for our mental and physical health to constructively ventilate our anger or act it out in one way or another. This is an important and valuable step in our growth. Giving ourselves permission to express our feelings helps us get in touch with them so we can deal with them. Expressing helps us heal childhood scars.

Aggressively expressing our negative feelings (without taking responsibility for creating them) is distinctly better than suppression—but it can still create many problems. Instead of getting ulcers, we "give" people ulcers. (Of course, we can't *really* give someone an ulcer, but we can say and do things that trigger their demanding programming—which may in turn give them an ulcer.)

Expressing anger or frustration can backfire and become a destructive pattern in itself. Addictive mental habits get stronger with practice! We may turn into time bombs ready to explode whenever someone pushes our addictive buttons. When we fly off the handle with rage, we have the illusion that the world is making us upset—and that we are victims of "mean" people. The truth is that we're victims of our own programming. And we are trapped in mental sets that make us throw people out of our heart with righteous indignation.

Although lashing out at others temporarily vents the steam and ensures that we are in touch with our feelings, we run the risk of expressing in a way that strengthens blaming programs in our minds. We may feel relaxed after a particular explosion. However, we still have the addictive demands that make us vulnerable to similar situations in the future. And love is tarnished when we blame our partner for our own sad or mad feelings.

Many people express their feelings using the pressure cooker method. They build up their emotional steam until they're ready to explode. And then like Mount Saint Helens it spews all over. It's more skillful to sincerely share your feelings as they arise inside you—observing them with interest. Expressing can be done with clarity, firmness, love, and gentleness.

But isn't there a next step beyond skillful expression that can open the door to an even higher level of harmony and happiness?

The Most Skillful Way

We're in a dilemma. The dilemma is that we feel separate and unhappy when we *suppress* our feelings. And our partner may trigger their addictive demands when we *express* our anger, irritation, or resentment. Either way there's turmoil. How do we get out of this trap?

> *There is a next step in personal growth beyond suppressing or expressing. When we reprogram an addiction into a preference, we eliminate the direct cause of our upset—our demand. Then we no longer create a separating feeling to either suppress or express. Instead of dealing with the symptom (our fear, frustration, or anger), we get rid of the cause (our demand). This offers us the best life possible.*

In other words, by turning a demand into a preference, the problem of suppression or expression doesn't come up. We've removed the *cause* (our demands) and not just dealt with the *effects* (anger, fear, etc.).

When we get in touch with strong emotions, the adrenaline in our blood stimulates us. If we don't let the separate-self ego run away with a couples boxing match, we can use this energy instead for our personal growth. For example, when you next feel angry, you may choose to begin saying the Twelve Pathways to yourself. Repeat them over and over, if needed.

> You will notice how your anger and irritation can drain away as you turn the adrenaline rush into on-the-spot inner work.

Let's clearly understand that until you transform your addictions to preferences, your personal growth requires that you *learn to express your feelings.* You can't play it phony and pretend you don't have addictions when you really do. This slows your growth.

Opening Up the Real You

The feelings you wish to hide are not a part of the real you. They are simply triggered by programs in your mind. As you grow in awareness, you'll be able to watch your mind trigger these programs—*but you will no longer identify yourself with them.* You will simply see them as the runoff of mental sets or programs that were put into your mind in times past. You don't need to addictively reject your unpleasant tapes—but you don't have to run them the rest of your life, either.

Now let's return to Connie's overeating problem. For years, Connie suppressed many of her feelings—including the good ones. As a child, her mother did not allow her to express her feelings. "Don't you dare say that to me. Go wash your mouth out with soap!" This led to her compulsion to overeat. At least she could feel something—even if it was only momentary satiation from stuffing herself. Luckily for Connie, she eventually understood that she was sabotaging herself and her relationship with Rick.

Her next step was to allow herself to express her feelings. She joined a support group that gave her a safe place to begin opening up. At first it was difficult. Gradually she began to feel all the anger and shame she was holding inside—and to express it. Finally, the dam burst and her feelings came forth with a flood of tears that should have been shed many years before.

She ultimately got the courage to share her problem with Rick. In many emotional sessions, she opened herself to him and began to share more and more. Often her sharing was not as skillful as it could be. She expressed much grief—often in a blaming way. However, it was a step in the right direction. At least she was no longer holding it all inside where it was festering and destroying her mental and physical health, not to mention her relationship.

After Connie began to share her anguished feelings of shame and anger, she gradually learned skills to help her use the energy from those feelings for her personal growth. She got more and more in touch with all the demanding programming she had been harboring throughout her life. She progressively changed many of her addictions into preferences. She no longer demanded that Rick see her in a certain way, or that she not have an eating disorder. She practiced loving and accepting herself.

Feelings of inner peace blossomed in her and increasingly she experienced a life of fulfillment, inner and outer honesty, and joy. Eventually her eating disorder died away. Her relationship with Rick moved into levels of love and intimacy she had never before dreamed possible.

Communication Without Blaming

When you communicate your deepest feelings, you don't have to put on a dramatic Hollywood act. Just share openly and nonaggressively, if possible. We use the term "sharing" to mean opening up and letting someone know your deeper feelings and thoughts. When you do it, it's like taking a load off your back.

> *Sharing helps you find the "us" place behind the differences between you and your partner.*

Unskillful sharing blames, accuses, demands, and insists that you are right and the other person wrong. Unfortunately, these can take place when sharing. But it's still sharing, and may provide a next step beyond dead silence. Sharing is just not hiding anything.

It may take you a while to develop your skill in sharing most effectively. Begin to notice when you fall into erroneous blaming statements like "You make me so frustrated because you. . . ." Use statements that clearly indicate *your* responsibility for your own experience, such as "I make myself frustrated because my programming demands . . . (tell what you want)."

When you share, you consciously express your feelings. It's as though you invite your partner to "look at what's happening in me." Sharing opens the door for both of you to communicate about your inner worlds together—preferably with understanding and compassion—and with insights into the inner work yet to be done. Sharing can set the stage for eventually changing an addictive demand to a preference. Sharing does not necessarily require either of you to agree about who's "right" or "wrong."

Sharing With Love

Hiding your deeper feelings keeps you trapped in a world of separateness. Breaking through your hesitation to communicate more honestly is one of the fastest ways to open your life and your heart to your partner.

When Penny and I began our partnership, she told me whenever I had bad breath, which was frequent. No one around me had previously mentioned it. But Penny was determined to create a deep level of emotional honesty in our relationship. So she fearlessly mentioned my bad breath whenever she noticed it. I did not find this news pleasant. However, I was able to accept it emotionally. I knew that when she was open and honest about this, it was more relaxing to her than stewing inside and not mentioning it. And better for our relationship. Sometimes just sharing about something we don't like can defuse the unpleasant emotions—even though we still wish it didn't exist.

I began looking for a solution. Eventually I found that if I took a half teaspoon of sodium bicarbonate 30 minutes after eating, my food would be digested more thoroughly. Bad breath is now quite rare. Penny's willingness to share enabled her to feel better, and helped me improve my health. More honesty and less "diplomatic politeness" brings us closer together.

It is difficult to have a high level of trust in your relationship if you do not share your feelings. Your partner won't know where you're at—and may suspect the worst. Here's the way this was expressed in a workshop:

> The basis of a relationship is our willingness to share. What happens when we share is that we

discover our mutual realities—mutual goals, mutual games, you might even say. We find that "us" place behind all the differences. We start looking for similarities as opposed to differences. When we reach that point, what we're doing is building trust with one another.

No relationship can exist without trust. And then there's that constant, threatening grating of your addictions. What you'll find is that when the addictions start running high, you'll pull back your involvement if there is no trust. So what you're doing in a relationship—with the communication, with the shared reality—is that you're building a safe place or a place of trust. And from that comes the cooperation in the present and in the future—the commitment to each other's well-being and to sharing life together.

In the rocky confrontations that life can throw at your relationship, both of you may attack each other with various addictive demands. Your relationship may suffer unless a *deep level of trust* has been built up by open communication.

|| *Living truth produces alive relationships; operating behind a phony mask deadens your relationship.*

By communicating honestly on deeper and deeper levels, you are building a bond that unites your hearts and minds. You increasingly treasure the loving energy that flows every day between you and your partner.

You deeply want your partner to enjoy high self-esteem and self-confidence. You want your partner to enjoy life to the fullest. And you are enriching your relationship by including your partner in your sense of self.

9

Ask for What You Want, but Don't Be Addicted to Getting It.

Your separate-self ego can create the illusion that if your beloved were really attuned to you and loved you as you think they "should," they would always know exactly what you're feeling and what you want. But do you always know exactly what's in your partner's mind and heart? It's best to assume that neither you nor your partner is a consistently accurate mind reader.

We usually create problems when asking for what we want. We may think it's not OK to want what we want, and our egos may create a separating me-*vs.*-you experience. There are two errors we can make when asking people to give us something or to do something for us. We may try to intimidate them and come on like a ten-ton truck with heavy right-wrong, fair-unfair, good-bad judgments to coerce them into feeling shame or guilt if they don't give us what we want. Or we may retreat into our shell and drop subtle hints of our martyrdom. We clam up, hoping the other person will give in.

Neither aggression nor retreat helps us play the game of life in a fun-filled way. As a way of breaking through the separate-self, let's learn to simply ask for what we want. And we then notice whether we have an addictive demand or a preference.

Sometimes when you ask your partner for what you want, you may make yourself feel apprehensive or fearful if you expect it will trigger your partner's anger or resentment. We call this "buying in to your partner's addictions." When you take responsibility for your partner's reactions, you enable both of your egos to get trapped in an enmeshed, codependent game.

I grew up in a family that did not make it OK to express feelings. I felt responsible for how others felt around me. Little Ken learned to be quiet about certain things—or at least to be careful how he dealt with them. When I was around 50 years old and really got into personal growth, I learned I did not have to take responsibility for other people's feelings. It felt like a breath of fresh air. I learned to simply ask for what I wanted in a matter-of-fact way without buying in to how another person might trigger their addictive demands. A popular book says, "It's OK to be me." That applies to all of us, which means it's also OK for you to be you.

Don't Buy In to Your Partner's Stuff

Once you stop buying in or assuming responsibility for your partner's emotions, you will begin to feel relaxed and peaceful when your partner goes through their addictive storms. If you can feel with loving compassion the "problem" of your partner without getting caught up emotionally in their predicament, your partner will be spared trying to cope simultaneously with both your addictions and theirs. (See the Eighth Pathway on page 101.)

Not buying in to your partner's stuff does not mean that you're heartless or uncaring. You can empathize with your partner's unhappy feelings. Even though you know you're not *directly* responsible, your heart will feel understanding and love. From a place of caring and compassion (rather than fear or condescension), you may look for ways to help them bypass or find relief from their addictive snags.

Wisdom is a blend of head and heart. Your heart leads you to reach out with compassion, and at the same time, your head is clear about cause and effect—you did not cause their upset. A good motto is:

> *I'll ask for what I want.*
> *I'll enjoy what I get.*
> *I'll work on any difference.*

And, of course, "Work on any difference" refers to inner work on your own emotion-backed demands—not to addictively pushing your partner to make them do what you want.

Here's some good advice from one of our workshops:

> It doesn't mean that she loves you more if she always agrees with you. It has nothing to do with you. It's all a runoff of the other person's programming. You keep wanting to make everything that happens in a relationship personal. "It's me. . . . It's me. . . . It's me." And it has nothing to do with you. The only thing that has anything to do with you is what's going on in your head. What's happening to the other person and what's going on in their head is theirs. And if we can learn to let it be, and pick up what's ours and leave what's theirs, it makes the relationship a lot easier. But we're so busy cleaning up after them. . . .

Asking With Love

Often we ask for what we want in a way that implies blame or a right-wrong judgment if our partner doesn't give us what we ask for. "You mean you won't even do this for me?" Or we may think, "I've been real courageous and up-front by asking for what I want, and you'd better reward me."

A more skillful and unifying approach is to ask for what you want with a calmness that shows you are not addicted to getting it. You might ask yourself:

- Am I trying to make my partner feel bad if they say "no"?
- Am I making a preferential request so my partner will not feel pressured?
- Am I feeling love when I ask for what I want?

Heart-to-heart love can shine through as your preferences gradually replace the demands that keep your relationship heavy-handed, neurotic, and tense. The habit of unconditional love can help you develop more skill in asking your partner for what you want. *Ideally, when you ask for what you want, you are simply sharing a preferential choice.*

When your partner has love in their heart, they'll freely give you everything they can afford to give—without the backlash of feeling resentful. That's it—for now. You're getting all that's gettable without activating their separate-self me vs. you.

That's why this guideline recommends that you ask for what you want—but don't demand it. Love in your heart will almost always bring you more happiness than getting what you want. And the power of love may give you both.

10

*Work on
Your Own
Personal Growth—
Not Your
Partner's.*

Some of us have a pile of addictive demands as big as Mount Everest, and some of us have smaller mountains to conquer. As we become skillful at recognizing our demands and begin making them into preferences, we can enjoy our journey with more energy, increased perceptiveness, and a lot more love.

Don't Hammer on Your Partner's Addictions

Let me warn you about something that can greatly retard your progress—or even blow up your relationship. Your separate-self ego may try a diversionary strategy that does not require it to surrender any territory.

> *It is easier to make a big deal out of your partner's addictive demands than to work on your own. Your ego often chooses to forget that your happiness depends on your growth, which is entirely in your hands— or your head!*

Personal growth is not like a game of checkers in which two people have to know the rules and agree to play together. The guidelines in this book offer you a way to *work on yourself.* They show you how to use the parade of situations in your life for your own growth. Your growth does not require that your partner be doing the same thing—although it's nice when that happens. Your partner doesn't even have to understand what you're doing. Your inner growth depends *only on you.*

You can delay your growth for many years (or even a lifetime) if you insist on criticizing, analyzing, and pointing out the emotion-backed demands of your partner. Your ego knows that the best way to defend its own demands is to attack. Such an aggressive attitude toward your partner's addictions permits you to ignore the need for your own inner work.

For your own growth, work on your demands and let everyone else (including your partner) take responsibility for their growth—or lack of it. And remember, you may actually grow faster if your partner behaves in ways you dislike—provided you use those opportunities for your own growth!

Many years ago when Penny and I first got together, I was busy giving a one-month training. One of the students, Claire, was particularly adept in working on addictive demands that arose day by day. As her teacher, I chose to give her many compliments on how well she was doing. And I would often hug her, as well as the other students—both men and women.

Although Penny and I were in a monogamous relationship, Penny's programming made her feel threatened and jealous when I gave any attention to Claire. My first response was to trigger a demand that Penny not feel challenged or jealous. From my point of view, there was really nothing happening that would justify her jealousy. I wanted to be only with Penny as a relationship partner. Eventually my separate-self led me into such thoughts as, "This is embarrassing. Here I'm teaching these students unconditional love and my partner is creating jealousy. We should be able to model what we are teaching."

But these demanding thoughts were only flickers through my mind. I'd had years of practice using the Living Love methods, and I instantly became aware

96

of the programming that was running in my mind. I caught my ego as it began slyly sliding into righteous judgmentalness: "I'm going to convince Penny why she shouldn't be jealous." Then my unified-self began to notice many options I had in this situation. I'm glad I didn't jump in and try to force Penny to drop her addiction. Instead, I had the good sense to work on myself. I decided I would not self-defensively point out that Penny had no reason to feel jealous.

Whenever she felt jealous, I made it a point to increase my expression of love and caring for her. If it was convenient, I'd put my arm around her and just *experience* what a beautiful person she was and how much I appreciated being with her. I told myself that the power of unconditional love would probably help her reprogram her jealousy—and it would take time.

And that's exactly what happened. She gradually began to feel comfortable when I worked with female students. Over the years, our trust and unconditional love for each other has grown so strong that her program causing jealousy has long since retired.

The inner work I had done was paying off for me. Bonita's jealousy had been one of the issues that had made me want to leave my second marriage. And now I was able to get off this position before it turned into an issue between us.

It is helpful to remember that your growth does not require you to rescue your beloved from their upsetting demands. You can't. Ultimately, each person must rescue himself or herself.

The real growth game of life is to learn to love everyone unconditionally—including yourself. Your own jealousy, fear, or anger is simply the "grist for the mill" of your personal growth.

The Two-Handed Approach

Most people are trying to get their relationship to work with one hand tied behind their back. Their main way of dealing with something they don't like is to blame their partner for their discomfort, make themselves a victim, and demand that their partner change. Our various guidelines suggest going beyond this demanding stance to a preferential position. This applies even if your partner is into alcohol or drugs.

How can this two-handed approach work if your partner is an alcoholic? On one hand, you try to change the situation. You can confront your partner and try to get them to seek help, perhaps with Alcoholics Anonymous. On the other hand, you do the inner work to free yourself from any addictive demand that keeps you in a fearful, judgmental, or morally superior attitude toward your partner. You dislike the programming—but keep a loving compassion for your partner.

So you deal with your life using two hands. With one hand you alter the situation, if possible; with the other hand you change your own addictively demanding program. If you're determined and skillful in doing the inner work, the latter will always work! The former, which depends on your partner's changing, may or may not work. Good luck!

The Ninth Pathway encourages us: "I act freely when I am tuned-in, centered, and loving, but if possible I avoid acting when I am emotionally upset and depriving myself of the wisdom that flows from love and expanded consciousness." Rare emergencies may require us to act immediately—and do our inner work later. But most life situations give us an opportunity to begin our inner work so that our actions may be wiser—and thus more effective.

Working on Your Own Programming

I've been amazed at the subtle way my ego makes me think I have a preference when I'm really running a demanding tape. How do I tell them apart? If I can explain what I want and why I want it without suppressing or getting upset inside, it's probably a preference. If I begin clouding up inside, it's a demand. I can notice this as I consciously take stock of what I'm feeling at the moment.

You may have to constantly confront your ego: Is it more important to create my inner experience of unconditional love for my beloved, or to try addictively forcing them to do what I want? Is what I'm demanding really worth stirring up so much hurt, anger, and separation between us? Do I really think my partner likes to live with someone who is constantly nagging and pressuring? Or pointing out their addictions? Is the pain and suffering I trigger in myself and my loved one worth the concession I might be able to force upon my partner? How long do the emotional wounds I create in myself take to heal at my present level of skill in changing addictions to preferences? Is the thing I'm wanting really worth the risk of diluting my love for my partner?

A Daily Practice

Here is a daily practice that can help you enrich your relationship with your beloved—and yourself:

1. **Read Personal Growth Books:**
Each day slowly and meditatively read five pages in *Handbook to Higher Consciousness* or *Gathering Power Through Insight and Love.* They are packed with information and techniques for creating a conscious, loving life. Reading them over and over can help you apply the guidelines in this book. You will also find it helpful to reread this book several times to help you get behind your ego's resistance to applying it in your daily life. And there are many other excellent personal growth books available.

2. **Use the Twelve Pathways:**
Memorize the Twelve Pathways and say them before arising and after going to bed. The Pathways give you handy condensed wisdom from thousands of years of human experience. They can be used as tools to help you accelerate your personal growth. They will gradually awaken the power of unconditional love. You may experience a noticeable internal shift if you say them slowly to yourself at times when you're upset.

   We especially recommend filling in the daily pages of *Handbook to Higher Consciousness: The Workbook,* which offers you practice in using the Twelve Pathways and other methods. Penny and I have written this workbook to give you the benefit of our many years in applying these practical techniques to enrich our lives.*

3. **Share Your Inner Feelings:**
Before going to bed at night, take a few minutes to develop insight into your addictive demands by sharing with your partner. As emphasized in Chapter 8, communicating on deeper levels with

* Described on page 197.

The Twelve Pathways
To Unconditional Love and Happiness

Freeing Myself

1. I am freeing myself from security, sensation, and power addictions that make me try to forcefully control situations in my life, and thus destroy my serenity and keep me from loving myself and others.

2. I am discovering how my consciousness-dominating addictions create my illusory version of the changing world of people and situations around me.

3. I welcome the opportunity (even if painful) that my minute-to-minute experience offers me to become aware of the addictions I must reprogram to be liberated from my robot-like emotional patterns.

Being Here Now

4. I always remember that I have everything I need to enjoy my here and now—unless I am letting my consciousness be dominated by demands and expectations based on the dead past or the imagined future.

5. I take full responsibility here and now for everything I experience, for it is my own programming that creates my actions and also influences the reactions of people around me.

6. I accept myself completely here and now and consciously experience everything I feel, think, say, and do (including my emotion-backed addictions) as a necessary part of my growth into higher consciousness.

Interacting With Others

7. I open myself genuinely to all people by being willing to fully communicate my deepest feelings, since hiding in any degree keeps me stuck in my illusion of separateness from other people.

8. I feel with loving compassion the problems of others without getting caught up emotionally in their predicaments that are offering them messages they need for their growth.

9. I act freely when I am tuned-in, centered, and loving, but if possible I avoid acting when I am emotionally upset and depriving myself of the wisdom that flows from love and expanded consciousness.

Discovering My Conscious-Awareness

10. I am continually calming the restless scanning of my rational mind in order to perceive the finer energies that enable me to unitively merge with everything around me.

11. I am constantly aware of which of the Seven Centers of Consciousness I am using, and I feel my energy, perceptiveness, love, and inner peace growing as I open all of the Centers of Consciousness.*

12. I am perceiving everyone, including myself, as an awakening being who is here to claim his or her birthright to the higher consciousness planes of unconditional love and oneness.

---

* The Seven Centers are Security, Sensation, Power, Love, Cornucopia, Conscious-Awareness, and Cosmic Consciousness.

inner honesty is essential to a healthy, vital relationship. It is important to acknowledge your addictions during this sharing. Don't play teacher by working on your partner's head. Avoid your ego's tendency to tell your partner how "wrong" they are. Pinpoint specific emotions and addictions *you* experienced during the day. Remember to use "I" language, such as "I felt hurt when you . . ." instead of "You hurt me when you. . . ."

Many people have found they get better results when they use this form:

> *I create the experience of*
> _____
> *(specify your emotions)*
> *because my programming demands*
> _____.
> *(state what's happening)*

What is your separate-self wanting to hide? Share it. Which of the Twelve Pathways applies to each of your addictive demands today? Use it. How could you communicate more of the love you feel? Do it.

Ask your partner how they feel. Ask specifically what you could do this month to improve your relationship. If your partner is not available or does not want to participate, write what you are telling yourself in a diary, or share with a close friend, making sure you take responsibility for your experience.

Be kind to yourself and don't use the process of changing your addictions to preferences as another way to criticize or reject yourself or your partner. See it as a challenging growth game (played out by your separate-self and your unified-self). This game offers the greatest of rewards—the creation of more heart-to-heart love, and the joy of living.

11

Notice That Both You and Your Partner Always Have Beneficial, Positive Intentions.

Perhaps for many people the happiest time of their lives was when they first fell in love. This romantic love was based on a longing for a loving partner—and it was great while it lasted! For most of us, the illusory bubble burst as our daily lives triggered addictive demands that we did not know how to handle.

The usual experience is that romantic love cannot be maintained. After a bitter breakup, some people give themselves programming that makes them cynical about love and relationship: "Men just want your body," or "Women are totally irrational," or "I'm not going to put myself through the wringer again."

I've had my share of romantic love—and it was really great. And I feel that I've had more than my share of a broken heart following romantic love—and it was really awful. The intense feelings of romantic love—even though based on an illusion—still stand out as one of my most exhilarating experiences when I look back on my life. When this relationship came crashing down, I wallowed in a mire of misery that took me many months to recover.

Keeping Love Alive and Growing

Soon after this crash, a gradual opening on my part allowed me to learn from several wise people who passed through my life. An understanding eventually grew in me which evolved into the Living Love methods. The basics of this system are laid out in the guidelines of this book.

I have now had the experience of living with my third wife, Penny, for 11 years (as of 1990). Our romantic feelings of love have grown year by year. The age-old maxim that deep levels of love and romance are not sustainable does not apply in our experience as we use the Living Love methods for unfolding our lives together.

In Chapter 3 we examined how our demands create alienation. Penny and I have found the demand/preference principle to be essential in helping us create our shared happiness. This insight has enabled us to pinpoint our addictive demands and work toward changing them to preferences. Applying these guidelines has helped us avoid crystallizing our addictions into strained issues that create separateness between us. We use them to take responsibility for our own feelings, and to avoid blaming either ourselves or the other person for our own fears, frustrations, or angers. These guidelines also help us uncover our subconscious, dysfunctional inner child programmings. We still have unfinished inner work. And the personal growing we have done so far has enabled us to create a joyous adventure together.

Your Beneficial, Positive Intentions

This chapter will share with you another vital guideline that Penny and I use. The longer we're together, the more we appreciate it. It leads us to insights that keep giving us a deeper love and unity. We call it the Second Wisdom Principle:

Behind it all, we always have beneficial, positive intentions (even though we may sometimes use unskillful ways to achieve them).

As you learn to apply this vital principle to your life, "miraculous" things may begin to happen in creating a relationship nearer to your heart's desire. You will discover that both you and your partner are basically good—*always!* Even when you do unskillful things! This awareness helps avoid crunching each other's self-esteem and self-confidence.

Let's look at this guideline carefully so you can apply it in your life. It says that your partner has beneficial, positive intentions behind all their actions you may despise. Your partner's addictive programming might have led them into terribly unskillful behavior. However, every addictive demand is motivated by a positive intention. Always, *without exception*, they've had good intentions behind their unskillful actions!

Don and Marcia have trouble seeing each other's beneficial, positive intentions. Marcia just purchased an expensive dress that their budget can't afford. She feels guilty about the dress but won't discuss her feelings with Don. And to top it off, she flirted with Tim at the Christmas party. Don, on the other hand, won't confront Marcia about the expensive dress. He feels resentful and angry. When he sees Marcia flirting with Tim at the party, he swiftly schedules a luncheon date with Barbara, who works in the office next to him. Marcia finds out and is livid. Don refuses to discuss it with her. She reacts by refusing to have sex with him for a month.

From Don's point of view:

> It's nonsense to think that Marcia always has beneficial, positive intentions behind everything she does or says. We've been hard up for money and she goes out and buys an expensive new dress we can't afford. What's positive about that? And what could possibly be positive about her flirting with Tim? She

just wants to punish me. And she's trying to hurt me by not having sex with me for a month! What's beneficial about that?

From Marcia's point of view:

How could Don have beneficial, positive intentions when he won't even talk with me about what he's feeling? He just mopes around, sullen and depressed, as though he's carrying the weight of the world on his shoulders! No wonder I want a new dress. He's away all day and then he ignores me all evening—that is, until bedtime. What's positive about his wanting sex time after time when he knows I don't feel like it? And what about his "innocent" luncheon date with Barbara? He won't even talk with me about it. That's not positive or beneficial. Obviously, his only motive is revenge for my harmless "fun" with Tim.

Aren't these exceptions to the guideline that our partner always has beneficial, positive intentions? No! Let's find out why:

First, exactly what do we mean by "beneficial, positive intention"? *A beneficial, positive intention is a desired internal experience* that you really want behind a surface goal; it is an image, thought, or feeling that is conducive to your well-being.

> *Whatever you do or say is ultimately motivated by your intention to bring about an internal experience that you desire.*

This is true for everyone. All of us have similar positive intentions—and we sometimes may try to achieve them in unskillful ways that don't work well. ("Unskillful" refers to ineffective or harmful efforts to get what we want.)

Here is a partial list of possible internal experiences that motivate everything that you or your partner says or does.

To experience myself as:

acceptable	fulfilled	prosperous
accepted	fun-loving	relaxed
accepting	genuine	reliable
acknowledged	happy	responsible
alive	healthy	responsive
appreciated	helpful	safe
attractive	humorous	satisfied
beautiful	important	secure
calm	independent	sexual
capable	intelligent	sexy
comfortable	joyful	strong
competent	knowledgeable	supported
complete	lovable	supportive
confident	loved	valuable
dependable	loving	valued
energetic	nurtured	worthwhile
enthusiastic	nurturing	worthy
excited	peaceful	and many more!

How Does It Work?

Now let's practice using the previous incident with Don and Marcia. If Don is open to exploring possible positive intentions behind the things Marcia has done, he might ask himself:

What could be the beneficial, positive intention behind Marcia's "wasting money" when she knows the budget can't afford it? Does she have the beneficial, positive intention to feel *prosperous?* Or *joyful?* [If possible, Don could simply ask her directly and not guess.]

And her flirting with Tim at the Christmas party. Perhaps Marcia wanted to feel *attractive* or *accepted.* What is her positive intention behind turning off sex for a month? It could be that her positive intention in this case is to feel *appreciated* or *valued.* I don't even remember the last time I thanked her for something she'd done.

When Marcia tries to discover Don's beneficial, positive intentions, she may make these observations:

What are Don's positive intentions behind not talking to me and sulking around the house? Perhaps Don won't talk to me about the dress because he wants to feel *safe* or *relaxed*, or to see himself as *independent*.

And maybe behind his wanting sex all the time is a desire to hear inside that he's *capable* and *fulfilled*. The lunch with Barbara could have been his way of trying to get his positive intentions. And I guess I haven't been doing anything to help him boost his self-esteem lately.

Suppose either Don or Marcia won't talk to the other. Even if they aren't able to find out for sure what each other's positive intentions are, just knowing that beneficial motivations are there helps them find more understanding and compassion than they had to begin with.

Now check again the list of possible positive intentions on the preceding page. Get a sense of which intentions may apply in actual situations behind the soap opera of your own daily events. No matter how big the battle with your partner, both of you have only been trying to achieve a positive experience: to feel more accepted, more acknowledged, more capable, more complete, more confident, more joyful, more relaxed, more satisfied, more secure, more sexy, more worthwhile, more loved or lovable, etc.

Exploring your partner's possible positive intentions can enable you to stay aware of the basic goodness of your partner—and keep unconditional love alive in your heart.

Make a copy of the list of possible positive intentions to keep with you. Add to it. Refer to it when your separate-self ego is ranting and raging and making you feel unhappy. Apply this "first aid" to your bleeding emotions to help you get in touch with your unified-self programming—which is out of reach at the moment!

Distinguish Between Goals and Intentions

Be careful not to confuse goals with beneficial, positive intentions that motivate our goals. For example, to lose 20 pounds is a goal; the positive, beneficial intention (desired internal experience) may be to hear inside that you're attractive. Getting a master's degree is a goal; the positive intention behind the goal might bc to see yourself as competent or intelligent.

How do you identify your positive intention? Just ask yourself what you would experience inside if you got what you want. When you go behind what you're doing or saying in the moment—*behind the goal* you're wanting to accomplish—you will recognize the reason for your goal. You are only trying:

1) to *see* yourself as, or
2) to *hear* inside that you're, or
3) to *feel*
   SECURE, COMFORTABLE, LOVABLE, ALIVE, STRONG, CAPABLE, WORTHY, or whatever.

A Deeper Understanding

This beneficial, positive intention guideline can help *you* understand your partner's desire to have the internal experience that they are acceptable, capable, or worthwhile—*intentions just like the ones you have for yourself!* Don't let your ego use the beneficial intention principle to accuse your partner of unskillful actions. You will lose its benefits if you misuse it as a way of criticizing or manipulating your partner. The separate-self ego will try to use anything it can to divert your attention from your own inner work!

> *The purpose of formulating your partner's positive intentions is to help YOU grow in understanding, compassion, and love for your partner.*

As you become aware of your partner's positive intentions, your unified-self may wonder what you can do to help your beloved experience their beneficial, positive intentions. Perhaps you can express your love more often from your heart so your partner can feel more loved and lovable. You can offer a safe space for them to share feelings. Can you creatively think of a unifying way that you can help them achieve their beneficial, positive intentions?

Can you discover your own beneficial, positive intentions behind something you're doing that is not working as you want? Can you find a more effective way to achieve your positive, beneficial intentions? Can you drop some addictive demands, and go more directly for the internal experience (your positive intention) you're really after? Perhaps to feel loved or lovable?

Remember that the purpose of the beneficial, positive intention principle is not to justify or defend unskillful acts. It's to help *you* achieve insights from a wiser perspective so *you* can make more effective decisions that unfold deeper levels of togetherness, love, and happiness with your partner. It's to help *you* remain mindful of the basic goodness we always have behind our sometimes unskillful actions.

You may also have to guard against your separate-self's attempt to abuse beneficial, positive intentions as another way to make your partner wrong. Don't say to yourself, "If my partner only understood that I just want to feel appreciated and loved, they wouldn't make such a big deal over what I did." Don't fall into this trap of using the concept of positive intentions to justify anything you do. Your actions have consequences. Use it to deepen your own understanding and improve your ability to love unconditionally.

Intentions Behind Intentions

Sometimes you may need to hunt for the beneficial, positive intention behind an action or goal. Let's take another couple as an example. Suppose Joan finds out that her husband John had an affair two years ago with their attractive neighbor. Suppose she feels hurt, enraged, and jealous and retaliates by depriving John of sex. Is this shutting off sex a beneficial, positive intention? Of course not.

Remember, a beneficial, positive intention is always *a desired internal experience—not an action or goal.* Suppose John asks Joan, "Why are you cutting off sex?" The answer is "I want to pay you back." Is revenge or "paying back" a beneficial, positive intention? No, it's still a separate-self *goal.* But John continues asking Joan, "Why do you want to pay me back?" She replies, "I want you to know how hurt I feel." He still hasn't discovered the beneficial, positive intention.

But John hangs in. He knows it's always there. He puts himself in her shoes and asks himself what might be motivating her. He guesses that the goal behind Joan's wanting him to realize her pain is for him to promise that he'll never have another affair. He asks her and learns that he has guessed right. And while it's an assurance he's willing to make now, he knows that what really matters is that she achieve the internal

113

experience of her underlying positive intention. He's confident that they can uncover it.

He asks Joan again, "If I promise that I'll never have another affair, what will you experience inside?" Eventually it boils down to something Joan wants to *see, hear, or feel inside.* In this case it is "I want to hear inside that I'm loved and important."

John will still have to grapple with his own internal demand that makes him feel guilty about the old affair. At the same time, his fresh understanding of Joan's positive intentions gives him a wider perspective on the situation. It stirs in him a desire to support Joan in her wish to feel loved and important. This reaches beyond his promise of fidelity.

He makes a commitment inside to cherish her as he did before they married. He doesn't realize that in doing so he's achieving the very beneficial, positive intentions behind his having the affair with the neighbor two years before: to feel alive and excited.

And now John has the key for turning a lemon into lemonade. Instead of demanding more sex, he can creatively choose to do things that may help Joan achieve her positive intentions: to hear inside that she's loved and important. Healing between them and within each of them has already begun and will continue. And, incidentally, this key to compassion may be the best way to restore their lovemaking.

No Exceptions

Smarting under the lash of your anger, frustration, or fear (created by your addictive demands), you may have mentally condemned the actions and words of your partner. Most likely, at those times you were unaware of the beneficial intentions motivating your partner's actions. You may have judged your partner's actions as "stupid" or "mean"—instead of looking for insights into their basic motivations behind the unskillful behavior.

Your separate-self ego enables you to forget that you and your partner are ALWAYS SIMILAR in your underlying intentions and motivations. These are generally to feel secure (whatever that means to each individual), to feel acceptable or accepted, and to feel loving or loved. You must use your imagination and insight to discover which beneficial, positive intentions might apply in a specific situation.

If your mind has self-critical and self-rejecting habits, you may be unaware of your own positive, beneficial intentions. Be sure to use this wisdom principle to stay in touch with your own basic goodness.

To Sum Up

There are beneficial, positive intentions behind all actions, including harmful, unskillful ones. For your personal growth, meet the challenge of finding them. They help you increase your understanding and unconditional love. They add to your effectiveness in getting through the rough spots with your partner— as well as yourself.

You can confirm an astounding fact: No matter what happens, the positive intention principle always applies. You are both always motivated by beneficial, positive intentions—even if you are one day from breaking apart! Behind it all, your partner is basically good. AND SO ARE YOU!

By developing your skill in discovering your own and your partner's beneficial, positive intentions, you can begin to cut through a lot of separating acts in the drama of your life together. You can greatly accelerate your growth. You can take giant steps toward happiness that you have never before found to be within your stride. You can bring the power of unconditional love into your life. You may enjoy the "miracle" of enabling your marriage to become more loving and satisfying each year you are together.

We have explored the life-enriching benefits of upleveling your addictive demands to preferences, formulating your beneficial, positive intentions, and discovering the basic goodness of both yourself and your partner. These are powerful tools for releasing the magic of unconditional love. And there's still more.

12

Give All the "Gifts" You Can Emotionally Afford to Give.

One way you can enhance the adventure of life with your loved one is to give all the "gifts" you can emotionally afford to give. We are not talking about gifts you can buy at a store. We mean giving of yourself. " The only gift," said Ralph Waldo Emerson, "is a portion of thyself."

This means increasing your flexibility by trying new ways. This does not mean trying something your partner wants because you "should" or because your partner won't like it if you don't. It means trying something your partner wants because you like giving "gifts" to your beloved. You do it from an internal sense of choice. It's a statement of your inner strength—of your generosity and your love.

One of the finest gifts you can give your partner is to help them experience themselves as beautiful, capable, and lovable when they are natural and relaxed. If your partner has any self-blaming tendencies, there will be times when you might genuinely say, "Yes, I know you don't like what you did and are rejecting yourself. I love you. Be gentle with yourself."

Increasing My Flexibility

My own life has been enriched by becoming open to experiencing things my coadventurer wants. One of the issues that often pushed some of my previous relationships into a cliff-hanging mode had to do with monogamy. I wanted to occasionally have sex with someone else, and my partner wanted otherwise. After years of striving to make it work, I had the wisdom to hunt for the way out.

I began to realize that the pleasure I got in sexual experiences outside the relationship was not as great as I had expected it to be. And it took so much energy and planning to bring these outside contacts into fruition—usually with so little fruit.

I also eventually noticed that most couples who were open to outside sexual activities did not stay together very long. Monogamy is not a guarantee of permanency—but it can be a great help. It simplifies the addictive demands that are triggered between two people. I finally decided to let go of my unworkable models and instead be open to the form my relationship offered. I made up my mind to give the gift of total sexual fidelity to my beloved.

Then I began to get more of what I really wanted—more love, trust, and emotional intimacy. Thus by giving this gift, I learned to bypass a swampy area in my life that I had sometimes got sucked into. By dropping my addictive demands for sexual variety, and focusing more energy into making the most of our *mutual* sexual energies, I found I could create far more unity with my partner and much less separateness—with more fun, too!

Giving Through Generosity

Our guideline suggests that you freely give your beloved all the "gifts" you can emotionally afford to give. Don't let your use of this guideline be confused by female-male polarities in our age of progress away from male chauvinism. "I won't give in on this! I have my rights!" We've heard the claims of some feminists that women are superior to men, and of some machos who think that men should dominate women. To me, the realistic approach is that men and women are alike in most ways and different in some ways. Each person has equal rights to decide their own lifestyle and destiny. No one has final answers to how we "should" manage our day-to-day activities—either individually or as a group. We are processes—and the world is a process.

The question is: Do we live together in a her-*vs.*-him struggle, or in a her-*and*-him cooperative, loving way? Our guideline says to give all the "gifts" you can afford to give. This works equally well for both sexes to bring the power of unconditional love into the life of the person who follows it.

Suppose I want one thing and my partner wants another. What do I do? I explore letting go of what I want; but I do not give a "gift" I cannot afford to give—because I'll resent it. I give with a feeling of inner strength that lets me go beyond compromise, defeat, or bartering.

It's sometimes difficult to accurately anticipate your limits. Pushing your limits is great for your growth and for your relationship—if you can handle it. If not, you can burn yourself.

Thus as our fifth guideline for creating a delightful relationship, I suggest that you build your relationship through making the choice to give your beloved all the gifts you can emotionally afford. I've found when I give generously without expecting anything in return, I feel an instant reward of internal satisfaction. And in one way or another, sooner or later I seem to get back more than I've given. This is a part of the magic of unconditional love!

13

Discover How Your Relationship Is Perfect for Your Enjoyment or Growth.

The guideline presented in this chapter has been previously mentioned. Understanding it is easy, but applying it consistently takes a lot of practice. The guideline points out that all the things you don't like about your life can be used for your growth. If you put a high priority on your personal growth, *you gain no matter what happens in your life*—even if it looks like you're losing!

If you and your partner are enjoying being with each other, life feels fine. And this positive experience is also great for your growth. It reinforces the program that your life together can be beautiful. If you're involved in a cat-and-dog fight, this too can be useful for your growth. It obviously does not add to your present enjoyment. But if you use this unpleasant experience to increase your skill in applying the various guidelines, you will add to your future enjoyment. You may not be able to change your partner, but *you can usually change your unpleasant emotional experience* of any situation.

This may mean focusing on the daily practice described in Chapter 10. Be sure to apply the two wisdom principles. Keep observing how the guidelines relate to your life.

The Most Frequent Obstacle

And now we get to the biggest problem you will find in your personal growth. The separate-self ego keeps blaming others (or yourself) for your fear, frustration, anger, and unhappiness.

> *Your ego will constantly pull you into the illusion that your experience reflects what's happening in your life—rather than the demanding or preferential programming you're using to perceive what's happening in your life.*

Although I've been teaching this principle for two decades, I find myself occasionally falling into this old trap. With the practice I've given myself over the years, I can usually catch my mind doing it within seconds or minutes after it begins to happen. And then I know that it's again time to do some inner work. I can use the situation to give me practice in getting free of my addictive perception of what's happening.

Lynn was convinced that her husband, Carl, was the cause of her unhappiness. She had so much to prove her "case." He drank heavily and was frequently put in jail for starting fights. With help from various sources, she eventually realized that while his programming created his unskillful behavior, he was not the cause of *her reaction* to it—her internal experience of unhappiness. She was unhappy because she was addictively demanding that he be different.

This insight was a major breakthrough for her. It helped her see her whole life differently No matter what the external events of her life were or how threatening they seemed, she now understood how her own programs directly created her upset feelings. And she still had to deal with Carl's behavior, hopefully with greater wisdom.

Our lives give us more than enough experiences to learn to skillfully use the guidelines. The problem is that we just don't use these opportunities for growth.

Instead of blaming our programming, we blame ourselves or others for the upsetting turmoil we feel. And this stunts our growth.

So we need to remind ourselves over and over again that whenever we're unhappy, life is just giving us a message we need for our growth. The Third Pathway may be used as a helpful reminder: "I welcome the opportunity, even if painful, that my minute-to-minute experience offers me to become aware of the addictions I must reprogram to be liberated from my robot-like emotional patterns."

This is difficult for many people to understand at first. Suppose you are married to a husband who physically or verbally abuses you or neglects you. How do you use this situation for your growth? To begin with, your programming led you to set up this partnership in your life. Perhaps your life is asking you to look at your programs that made you choose this person to be with. What was it that blinded you to your partner's programming? Did you have enough patience to learn about your partner's mental tapes before jumping into a commitment? Is your programming making you hold on to your partner when it's time to let go? Maybe your life is telling you to get help in dealing with some dysfunctional or codependent programming you picked up.

When you think you've got the message life has offered you, is it the most useful conclusion for your future happiness? If your separate-self ego comes up with a cynical message like "men are cruel and can't be trusted," you may be retarding your growth. The truth is that *people can always be trusted to live out their programming!* It's your job to discover their programming—before choosing involvement, if possible.

And it's your job to understand your own programming—and how it makes you relate to others.

The University of Life

Your life is ideal for your growth. Everything is a gift of the universe—even your shame, guilt, resentment, hatred, anger, fear, jealousy, or frustration.

> *It's as though the University of Life has set up the exact curriculum to offer each of us the lessons we most need to create happiness.*

By getting on with your practice using your daily life situations, you can win in the inner growth game no matter what happens. Your life is really set up to work—if you do.

The guideline in this chapter gives you some really good news. No matter what's happening, the situations in your life can be appreciated—*either for your enjoyment or for your growth!* And you can avoid the growth if you self-reject and blame yourself or your partner—and don't use the situation for practicing the guidelines. If you don't use it, you'll lose it.

Some people just *want to want* to work on their personal growth. Firm resolve is lacking. You will have achieved a great milestone when you can say to yourself, "I'm determined to use what I don't like in my relationship for my own growth."

You can dependably count on your programming to set up your life situations for practice in using these guidelines! You will perpetually attract experiences you need to change addictions to preferences. These experiences are the lessons you've signed up for!

Here's a message from one of our workshops:

The lessons are not going to change. What's going to happen is that you'll say, "I'm not going to take this.

126

I'm not going to deal with those lessons." And you go out and find somebody that really promises to follow the form you want. The whole world knows that's the way it's going to be. But because you had the addiction in your head, you will create your partner's violating it (or wanting to) every time you turn around. You will create it in your head because you hold on to the addiction. There's no place to work—but on your head. You can never get enough from the outside world—never.

Annette had a program that "all men are lazy." Her first husband reinforced that program perfectly. He had trouble keeping a job, and she struggled to support them both for four years. She finally left him in complete disgust.

Her second marriage would be different, she told herself. Although Byron had a steady job, he chose to spend his evenings and weekends playing his guitar and watching TV instead of doing the long list of household chores and yard work Annette had itemized for him. "I can't live with a lazy person like this," she said over and over to herself—and to him, usually with a burst of indignant anger. She was convinced that Byron was the cause of her increasing unhappiness, and she eventually left him with righteous disdain.

With her conclusion ("all men are lazy") fully established by "irrefutable evidence," she married Matt. Although amiable and gentle, he often left his shoes in the middle of the floor, didn't hang up his clothes, and rarely put away his tools. True to her program, Annette often blurted out to him that he was just like all the other men she had ever known—LAZY! She blamed him for her unhappiness and told him she simply couldn't live with such behavior.

She probably would have left him also and gone to her grave thinking that "all men are lazy" if she hadn't finally "caught" that it was her own internal program that was creating her reality and making her unhappy. She chose to consciously work toward emotionally accepting Matt the way he was. Whenever he left something lying around, she reminded herself that she could prefer—and ask—that he pick it up. And she could feel peaceful and accepting even if he didn't.

She also focused on the things he did that contradicted her program—such as the many weekends he selflessly spent helping his brother build a house. In time, she saw how a dysfunctional inner child program copied from her mother had undermined all her relationships and created many years of suffering for her.

Part of the beauty and perfection of your relationship is the way it helps you realize on deeper levels that your partner is not the direct cause of your irritation, fear, jealousy, or anger. The other person only helps you get in touch with your own internal models of how it all must be for you to let yourself enjoy your life. With this insight, you can more wisely decide whether you want to hold on to a particular program in your mind.

That which you experience as a source of pain in your relationship can really become a source of gain. Your relationship will constantly act as a mirror. You have the illusion of perceiving the other person. But what you are really seeing is both your own beauty and your own hang-ups reflected back to you.

Happiness Now

Since life is the way it is right now, empowering yourself to create the most love and happiness depends on the speed with which you can keep dissolving your demanding models of how it all should be. Your happiness depends moment by moment on your skill in emotionally accepting the ways things are.

In the split second of "now," you can do nothing to change a situation. So you can learn to relax your emotional muscles. You can usually enjoy what's now. And you can put energy into making any change you want in your world.

> *It is part of the perfection of life that, in the normal living out of your desire systems, you will automatically keep on the griddle that part of your addictive programming that is most raw and indigestible—and needs cooking.*

As your skill grows, so does your appreciation of your partner's contribution to your personal University of Life. Your ego had hoped that the relationship would be perfect for your enjoyment. But it forgot that enjoyment must be preceded by handling your programming that makes you vulnerable to such feelings as irritation, anger, shame, fear, frustration, guilt, jealousy, resentment, and boredom.

As you handle your addictive demands, you will increasingly experience the many ways both you and your beloved are beautiful, capable, and lovable. You will enjoy more profoundly the basic goodness of the relationship you've created. And the benefits of unconditional love will bloom in your life.

14

Enrich Your Relationship by Helping Others

Science tells us that about 4.8 billion years ago, planet Earth was formed from galactic dust from the big bang. In a warm saline ocean about 3.5 billion years ago, amino acids came together and eventually evolved into plants and animals. The dinosaurs came and went, perhaps wiped out by ecological changes following the dusty impact of a huge asteroid—similar to the global darkness predicted if we have an all-out nuclear war. Our apelike ancestors evolved about three million years ago, and our own species, *homo sapiens*, developed around 100,000 years ago.

You and I are pioneers in the cultural unfolding of humankind. Since our species began, there have only been an estimated 70 billion of us born—of which over five billion are alive today—about 7 percent! To put it in another way, in the last 100,000 years, there have only been perhaps 4,000 generations of human beings before us. I have personally known people from six of these generations in my own family!

Since our species is a remarkably brainy one, you and I are the beneficiaries of ideas, skills, and devices that have been contributed by countless people over the years. Our languages, books, arts, cultures, religions, philosophies, and technologies are gifts from our ancestors. Many people today have TV, cars, and medical attention that were not available even to the kings and queens of the past.

The organism we call Earth is being subjected to stresses that are terminating many species of life—

which like the dinosaurs will be gone forever. The air we breathe, the water we drink, and the nutritional quality of the food we eat is rapidly deteriorating.

Inside the boundaries of nations today, disagreements are settled by a three-part system of laws, courts, and enforcement. But among the 159 nations around the globe, international disagreements are settled *lethally*, rather than *legally*. Money urgently needed for food, housing, health care, education, and protecting the environment is spent on killing machinery to decide international disagreements with blood.

Our destructive commercial practices, our planet-raping lifestyles, and the international anarchy, which makes us settle disputes by the *law of force* instead of the *force of law* have now placed humanity on the growing list of endangered species.

Your Real Wealth

So what does all this have to do with the power of unconditional love? Like the Greek god Atlas, we can empower ourselves to take the world on our shoulders. The power of love can give you and me the energy, inner wealth, and even the time we need to play our part in creating a future for our children.

As you repair your dysfunctional injured child programming, as you release yourself from the tyranny of your addictive demands, as you notice the beneficial, positive intentions behind the unskillful acts we humans perpetrate on ourselves and others, as you attune to the basic goodness of every person, as you realize we're not our programming, and as you do the inner work needed to love everyone unconditionally—including yourself, YOU'LL BECOME A VERY RICH PERSON!

I'm not, of course, talking about wealth that can be deposited in a bank. I'm referring to the priceless inner wealth that we humans can give ourselves through personal growth: energy, insight, perceptiveness, love, wisdom, inner peace, joy, rapture in being alive, and a feeling of purpose in life. When you develop skill in applying the guidelines in this book, some of the inner wealth you gain will benefit your partner—although basically everyone must undertake their own journey of personal growth.

To the degree that you practice the guidelines presented here, your experience of life will be headed for a turnabout. You will increasingly experience love, fulfillment, and happiness that could not be bought for a billion dollars.

Through your personal growth that supports your body, mind, and loving spirit, you can become one of the "richest" on this planet. The power of unconditional love will give you a satisfaction that is otherwise unattainable. You will be experiencing most of the goodies that life can give you—*but not all.*

Finding the Highest Happiness

A human life concerned only with itself cannot create the highest happiness. The highest level of happiness in your relationship comes as you and your partner turn to helping others. This secret has been known for ages. Albert Schweitzer said, "One thing I know: the only ones among you who will be really happy are those who will have sought and found how to serve."

When we first embark on our journey of personal growth, our egos will be clawing for enough security to save us from our worst fears, enough sensations to

133

avoid the major frustrations, and enough pride, prestige, money, and power to protect us from our angers, resentments, and irritations. But we can never reach and sustain "enoughness" this way—for long.

So we face the growth toward which our lives are urging us. We encounter and contend with our wounded inner child and addictive programming. Like most learning, it's a zigzag process. As we gradually achieve a higher level of personal happiness, we are no longer incessantly preoccupied with *my* security, *my* sensation, or *my* power, pride, or prestige.

With the miracle of unconditional love, we discover we have surplus time and energy not needed to handle personal desires. Since our own inner demands are no longer insistent, our priorities of how we spend our time seem to spontaneously shift toward helping others. This lets our unified-self expand to a new dimension and depth.

We find our attention going outward, away from self-centeredness. We see how much suffering there is everywhere. There's a lot of healing needed, repair work to be done, and preventive programs to develop—in our neighborhood and all over our planet.

The social cooperativeness that flows when we love everyone as a brother or sister is needed to help solve the immense planetary problems we have created by living out our addictive, separate-self programs.

How Do We Help?

All of us have helped others at times. How do we grow in giving of ourselves? We can do something meaningful each day: a smile, a hug, a question that shows we care, a letter, an unexpected note, a heartfelt appreciation—or an anonymous helpful act.

We figure out, perhaps through a blend of intuition and common sense, what directions to take. We find a wise balance for supporting ourselves and giving to others. Generosity becomes a habit. We act as a conduit to sort things out and put them where they're needed.

We give some of our precious time! We give some of our precious energy! And we quietly give of our precious money to help support activities that help make this a better world for ourselves and our children.

The joys and benefits of giving come as our egos let go of programming that says, "I should give," or "I'm a good person if I give," or "People will like me more if I give." We give of ourselves simply because we live in a world that needs our help—*and we feel rich inside and find fulfillment in giving.*

Helping others does not necessarily refer to large-scale activities that are written up in newspapers. Each of us can find our personal ways that let us give what we can afford to give. We do what's for us to do—and leave the rest to others.

Penny and I know a grandmother in her fifties who lives in our area and has been working full-time at McDonald's for years. You can tell by her sparkling eyes and shining face that she means it when she says she's there to love and serve. Every day the staff and customers at that McDonald's get hugs. It may be that some of those people don't get affectionately touched or hugged anywhere else.

Depending on your approach, the work you do may be self-centered or it may be a way to help others.

It depends more on your inner motivations—*not so much on the type of work you actually do.* You could live out "another day, another dollar" programming in which people are objects from which you extract money. Or you could go to your job each day motivated by a wise balance between making money to live on and generously helping your customers. You may have discovered that when you open your heart to people and treat them as friends, the money will take care of itself. If you do your work while listening to your heart, you may even experience your "work" as "play."*

Loving and Serving

When you and your partner cooperate by increasingly giving to others, you open the door to an enrichment of your life together. It's another wonderful game to share. You will know that you are deeply *a part of it all.*

Regardless of the amount in your bank account, you are going beyond a "not enoughness" programming to a feeling of abundant inner richness. Your love and generosity affects an expanding circle of fellow humans. Ripples are set in motion. Service is love in work clothes.

The power of unconditional love will give you a wisdom and an open heart that can yield a lifelong joy of being alive. You will be helping humanity evolve from its present "me-*vs.*-you" programming. You will be helping to pass on the torch of civilization a little brighter than you received it. And you will be playing

* Treat yourself to *How Can I Help?* by Ram Dass and Paul Gorman (Alfred A. Knopf, 1985).

the part that the universe has provided for you to cooperate in humanity's graduating from the jungle.

In Summary

We have examined the seven guidelines for creating a delightful relationship. Now you've got the keys to living "happily ever after"—or at least knowing what the problems are! Skill in applying these guidelines in the storms of life is essential—and comes only with insights born from practice, practice, and more practice.

Since some relationships may go beyond the point of no return, the next section presents seven guidelines for altering your involvement—without sacrificing love. I hope you won't need these additional guidelines—but here they are if you do.

PART III

*Seven Guidelines
for Altering
Your Involvement*

15

*For Your
Own Growth,
Consider Staying
Involved Until
You Have Changed
Your Demands
to Preferences.*

We humans have a special ability to affect how we experience life. We can make problems for ourselves; we can solve problems. When we stand back and look at our lives from a panoramic perspective, we are capable of seeing that it is our addictive demands backed by dysfunctional inner child programming that keep us from enjoying our relationship.

You may be considering ending your relationship. Unless your life or health is in danger, just changing partners may not be all that helpful. Some people continually run away from life's challenges, blaming their partner or themselves; they create similar problems wherever they go. If you see recurring, unresolved themes in your life, you may want to ask yourself what part *your* programming is playing in them—and what you might do to heal or change the pattern.

You have your own particular pattern of addictively demanding how things should be. Chances are that when you settle in with a new person, in one way or another this programming, if left intact, will create problems in the relationship. So sooner or later you might as well battle your addictions to change them to preferences.

If your living together hasn't yielded happiness, take responsibility (without blaming yourself) for your experience. It's part of your apprenticeship in learning the lessons of your life. Don't unwisely throw away the opportunity for personal growth that a stormy relationship gives you. You can view this unpleasant (yet challenging and potentially growth-producing) turmoil as a gift from the universe. And all of us sometimes wish the universe weren't so generous with its gifts!*

Remember the University of Life discussed in Chapter 13? Your programming brought you together with your partner to help you learn what you most need to learn—whatever that is. And whether or not it feels that way to you right now, your partner is ideal for your personal growth—or your enjoyment. And you can't have the latter without the former.

Communicate Caringly

Your life is no doubt providing you with many opportunities to communicate with your partner. Share your gut-level feelings with the best skill you can—and don't be addicted to your partner's hearing your stuff without triggering some of their addictions. Keep working on your own programming to change your demands to preferences.

But if your addictions seem too rock-like, and after trying repeatedly, you just can't get on top of them, you may wonder whether you want to continue playing the game of living together. The situations in our daily lives offer us the fire that enables us to burn out our addictions. But this doesn't mean that you have to work so close to the fire that you burn yourself. The game is to cook your addictions—not you.

---

* My personal saga on using my "gifts for growth" is described in *Discovering the Secrets of Happiness: My Intimate Story*. It illustrates the saying "No pain—no gain."

16

*Alter Your
Involvement If You
No Longer Want
to Cooperate
in the Great
Adventure of Life.*

Your relationship offers you and your partner an opportunity to cooperate in the great adventure of life. When you lose the rapture of togetherness, a dullness, dutifulness, and dreariness can begin to set in. You'll hear your mind thinking, "Would it be better if we weren't together?"

Of course, your emotion-backed demands based on unfinished inner child injuries will be at the root of your troubles together. Changing addictions to preferences and becoming aware of beneficial, positive intentions behind unskillful actions may act like magic in clearing away clouds of separateness and dissension.

A very important part of your inner work is to emotionally accept yourself just as you are—addictions and all. Be realistic and face the fact that sometimes you can change addictions to preferences—and sometimes it may not happen when you want it to. Always be gentle with yourself. No one's perfect. You're a human being, and every one of us has inner work to do.

If month after month, one or both of you are unable to handle the separating interactions that are being created by childhood dysfunctions and addictive programming, and if you have lost your energy for cooperating, you may want to consider making changes.

Altering Your Involvement

Let's use the term "altering your involvement" instead of talking about ending the relationship.

145

Actually, there is no way to end your relationship with the person you've been living with. Children may keep you in contact with each other. But even if children, mutual friends, business associates, and in-laws aren't in the picture, residues of your experience together will continue in your mind as long as you live.

As fellow voyagers on planet Earth, you are in a relationship with everyone else on the earth. You breathe the same air, drink from the water supply of the planet, are warmed by the same sun, and are holistically related socially, economically, politically, culturally, environmentally, and otherwise. So, when seen from a global point of view, relationships cannot be totally terminated—they can only be altered in the quantity and quality of involvement.

There are two reliable ways to decrease the frequency and intensity of the upsetting turmoil that comes up with your partner:

1) change addictions to preferences, or

2) lower your involvement.

If your load of addictions feels too heavy and you feel too strained and stressed to effectively change enough of them, then you may decide to have less involvement. This usually means separating. And you still have the potential benefit of developing a warm lifetime friendship.

17

*Take Responsibility
for Altering the
Relationship—
and Don't Blame
Yourself or
Your Partner.*

Remember that your programming led you to play your part in setting up the relationship, determined how you lived in it, and is now playing its part in altering the involvement. Try to understand that the other person is not doing it to you. You are each creating your own experience of what is happening. Each of you plays an interrelated role of acting and reacting to your own and each other's demands and preferences. You are both co-creators of your reality together.

It will help if you don't give in to rationalizing to make you right and the other person wrong, you fair and the other person unfair, you consistent and the other person inconsistent, you "good" and your partner "bad."

Our minds are great at encouraging our egos to feel superior with all this rationalizing, but that's not where the wisdom lies. Remember that your relationship has been a joint interaction between two people. Keep bringing your attention back to the real source of your shame, guilt, hurt, self-rejection, blame, jealousy, fear, anger, resentment, and other separating emotions—your own programming.

Altering Involvement Without Blaming

Why shouldn't you blame your former partner? You have a long list of grievances that proves how badly you've been treated. Try to remember that your partner is not their programming. So you can blame their programming. But where did this unskillful (even disastrous) programming come from? Most likely it was from parents, companions, and TV. But where did their programming come from? And so on and on. Blame is a waste of time.

What you need is not a scapegoat to blame; you need to figure out what to do next. And you'll need all the wisdom you can muster.

Altering your involvement will give you lots of practice in remembering that your partner is not their programming. Suppose your partner does things to physically, psychologically, or financially injure you. Can you stay in touch with the beneficial, positive intentions behind their unskillful actions? Can you stay attuned to the basic goodness of yourself—and your warring partner? Can your unified-self let you strongly dislike or even oppose your partner's actions and still keep your heart open to loving your partner? This can be a real test of your skill.

Cooling the Separate-Self

Your separate-self does not have to conduct a trial in your head—in which you play the part of lawmaker, prosecuting attorney, judge, jury, and executioner. It's not necessary to convict your partner—or yourself— of heinous "crimes" in order to make it OK to change the form of your involvement. Stay open to the messages your life is offering you. And no doubt there is a part of you that wants to be able to look back on what's happened and appreciate the beautiful things you've shared together. That too is programming— the unifying kind.

You don't have to vilify your partner in your mind so you can sentence them to banishment from your life. You don't have to turn this into a tragedy. You entered into the relationship—it was your choice. You can alter your involvement in the relationship if you don't want to cooperate together any longer. You can keep it simple, compassionate, and loving.

Mutual Cooperativeness

Altering the form of your relationship can be done with your unified-self. I'd like to share a beautiful letter I received from David W. McClure, a minister of the Unity Church of Truth. In this letter he communicated that he and his wife, Barby, were separating. Here's the letter:

Dear Friends,

One of my favorite phrases from Kahlil Gibran's book, *The Prophet*, is one that I use often in weddings I perform:

"But let there be spaces in your togetherness,
And let the winds of the heavens dance between you.
Love one another, but make not a bond of love:
Let it rather be a moving sea between the shores of your souls."*

Last month I shared with you the news that my wife, Barby, had decided to release herself from involvement in the church and seek her own career and identity elsewhere.

I must now share with you that we have reached a time in our marriage relationship where it has become necessary for us to "let there be spaces in our togetherness." After a great amount of time and prayer, we have decided in an atmosphere of love and mutual respect, to divorce.

---

* Reprinted from *The Prophet* by Kahlil Gibran with permission of the publisher Alfred A. Knopf, ©1923 by Kahlil Gibran; renewal, 1951 by Administrators, C.T.A. of Kahlil Gibran Estate and Mary G. Gibran.

As I write this letter I am reminded of something Eric Butterworth wrote: "Certainly in our vast experience in counseling, we (as ministers) have discovered that marriage partners do not always grow at the same rate or even in the same direction. One of the great confusions of our society is the assumption that two people will always and forever be able to force their lives into one mold."

Barby plans to remain in Spokane for the time being and pursue her new career. I trust that all of you who have been and are her friends and supporters will continue to give her your love and active friendship even through these changes in our personal lives.

I intend to continue as your minister and to give myself enthusiastically and wholeheartedly to serving you through this ministry.

Each of you is very special to Barby and me, and we want to thank you for the positive, loving thoughts and supportive prayers you have given us during this time of transition.

Lovingly in Unity,

David

So take responsibility for altering your involvement. You're running an addiction if you're blaming yourself or anyone else. Through your unified-self, you can welcome this opportunity to learn the lessons of life so that you will not have to repeat them. You can set your sights on using the power of unconditional love to play the separation or divorce game—with understanding, compassion, and perhaps serenity.

18

Be Totally Open and Don't Lie or Hide Things.

Your partner's trust in you is just as valuable in reducing involvement as when you are living together. Your own lying or hiding aggravates your feeling of alienation from your ex-partner. Vindictive strategies can dominate your mind and trigger your worst separate-self programming. And then you'll have to live with the consequences of what you've created.

> *No matter what's happening when you separate, you always create YOUR experience of happiness or unhappiness, beauty or ugliness, heaven or hell.*

In some cases, your addictions can make you re-interpret beautiful things that happened in the relationship and create a sourness in their place. And these illusions may give you paranoid programs that can diminish your next relationship. If you are open and honest and take responsibility for your experience, parting can happen with more harmony.

Work for Win-Win Solutions

If you can, work out the details so that both of you feel you win. Focus on the beneficial intentions, basic interests, and concerns of yourself and your partner— rather than the issues you are fighting about. Don't dig into trench warfare so everything is a me-*vs.*-you battle. Instead, do your inner work to hold on to a "me-*and*-my friend" way of looking at your drama.

There is a human, caring way to sort out whatever comes up as you decrease your involvement.

Susan and Ernie are getting a divorce. They own a house that neither wants to give up. Each one willfully clings to the position "It's my house and I want it!" After several heated quarrels about the issue, they stop talking to each other. The house sits vacant for over a year while Susan and Ernie stew in their addictive demands.

Finally, Susan receives a job offer in another city, which she wants to accept. She gradually loses interest in keeping the house—but she stubbornly doesn't share all these changes with Ernie. Ernie, on the other hand, wants it all resolved and is willing to compromise. Yet his anger and resentment toward Susan won't allow him to communicate with her. Acidic hatred gnaws on them. Time does not automatically heal the wounds.

Let's see how all this could have been harmoniously resolved if Ernie and Susan had the skills and desire to communicate in a win-win atmosphere. Susan sees that Ernie is not the cause of her unhappiness. She remembers that he always has positive intentions (she senses they are to feel secure and capable), and she wants to fulfill her positive intentions (to see herself as fair and loving).

Ernie, likewise, understands that his own programming is creating his internal experience. He's aware of Susan's positive, beneficial intentions. They communicate openly and honestly with each other to discover a solution that satisfies both of their interests and concerns. And the house issue is resolved in a climate that promotes cooperativeness in spite of the divorce. They sell it and split the money.

Achieving win-win solutions may mean lots of communication. Be open about how you feel—and especially what you feel troubled about. Don't let your pride get in the way. Support your unified-self by using this form when talking with your partner:

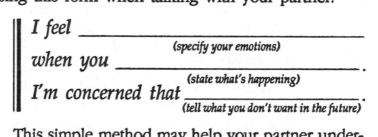

> *I feel* _____
> (specify your emotions)
> *when you* _____ .
> (state what's happening)
> *I'm concerned that* _____ .
> (tell what you don't want in the future)

This simple method may help your partner understand your feelings of fear, hurt, resentment, anger, shame, frustration, or loneliness. Together you may creatively examine possible alternatives to find a way you can both win. Try it and you may attain the previously unattainable!*

Above all, don't blame yourself for anything that happens. The clashing of your programming against your partner's programming has brought on your difficulties. There are life lessons in this for both of you. Here's some advice from one of our workshops:

> You set up a situation where both people win. No one has to lose when you don't make it a right-and-wrong game. Which means communication, which means getting agreements, which means being very clear and very straightforward—and very honest about what you want and what you're willing to give.
>
> There is security involved. No matter what we think, or think we think, there is some security threat felt on both sides—we have lived that way too long for there not to be. And there is a literal shock of thinking about parting and that brings up addictions

---

* See Chapters 17 and 18 in *Gathering Power Through Insight and Love* for more ways to skillfully and responsibly communicate how you feel and what you want.

that might have been buried for a long time. And that again is another reason why you want everything to be as clear, direct, honest, and open as possible. Because you're not dealing with just what is happening now. You're dealing with security aspects of however far back the relationship goes—and all the addictions that brings up. Which might literally have nothing to do with the here-and-now moment, but which we create as a "life and death" security situation. So it's drama-packed!

Don't turn your separate-self addictive demands loose to create bitterness and a closed heart. Do what you can to keep cooperation alive—at least on your end. All the details that need to be handled when two people decide not to live together any longer can become very complicated and sticky if trust and co-operativeness have been destroyed.

Life is giving you an opportunity for openness and generosity. Keep working to treat your ex-partner as you would treat a friend whom you love—and the rest of your life will be richer.

19

Follow Through on Your Commitments or Work Out a Change in the Commitments.

In your journey of personal growth, you start from where you are right now. And if where you are now involves such commitments as children or debts, you treat these as something established in your life, and you work with them.

Linda and Doug are parting. They own a furniture refinishing business together. Doug is furious that Linda wants full custody of their three children. He threatens to immediately desert their business and move to another state unless she changes her mind. Linda counters with a declaration that he will never get to see the children again if he abandons them and the business.

If they each follow through with their threats and renounce their commitments to their business and family, they may create years of agonizing strife that can destroy their happiness—and have a severely damaging effect on the well-being and security of the children.

Ignoring a commitment can lead your partner to feel that you've pulled the plug on their world. This may encourage cynicism, alienation, and distrust. And you and your partner probably have enough of that already. If you've made a commitment, your inner work may include carrying through with commitments unless you can renegotiate in one way or another.

Perhaps your life is trying to give you a message about making commitments too rapidly or too casually. Commitments always involve a claim on your future energy and time. You know that the world changes and your melodrama changes. On the other hand, some of the more worthwhile goals of life require that you make certain commitments. So you learn to find your path between too much and too little.

This is the way it was expressed in a Living Love workshop:

> Be honest about what you're willing to be there with—what you're willing to agree to. What I have found over and over is that people say they're willing to do more, give more, be more than they really are. And this lowers the trust. And you start perpetuating again that cycle of not being able to maintain a love space. It really doesn't matter what your agreements are. It really doesn't! What matters is that you're willing to be there with them in terms of either following through on them or communicating—renegotiating. And it's that communication that may keep that heart space open.
>
> It's like when I'm straight with a person, he or she knows this is how far I'll go—and exactly what I can do. Usually that person has the resources to be able to handle things up to that point. But when you promise to a certain point and you don't follow through on your agreements, it not only involves you. It involves the other person, it involves others that they're involved with, and it starts getting into a mad cycle of addictive programming that you have to straighten out somehow. So really be honest about what agreements you're willing to keep—and keep them or renegotiate them.

You honor your commitments (or mutually renegotiate) to create a more livable world, not only for others but also for yourself. Following through on commitments you have made is a way of increasing your self-esteem and loving yourself. For you will always have to live with yourself.

162

20

Hold On to Heartfelt Love, for Only This Will Enable You to Make Wise Decisions.

When you are decreasing your involvement in a relationship, you'll probably have many opportunities to work on yourself to keep love in your heart. You may have the challenge of understanding the beneficial, positive intentions of someone who is angry at you. Or perhaps you will get to test your skill with someone who tries to hit your addictions to target your feelings of guilt, shame, and hurt. Perhaps that person will lie or say bad things about you to your friends. Some of your strongest security, sensation, and power addictions that have only been lurking around your mind may jump out and tear at you.

And how about all the supporting actors and actresses in the drama of your lives? Each will have their set of "right-wrong" programmings they will gladly offer you for free. If you don't work to keep your head clear and your heart soft, you might buy in to others' opinions and become trapped in hatred, guilt, distrust, or "getting even." Decreasing your involvement is a great test of your skill in loving everyone unconditionally—including yourself.

If you addictively maintain that the only way to change your involvement is to "fight your way out," you set yourself up for unnecessary separateness and suffering. I remember reading about a divorce attorney who advised his client against the high cost of what he wanted to do. The client replied, "I don't care what it costs or even if it takes all my money, I just want to hurt her."*

When you act vindictively, you not only pay high legal fees, you can also lose the understanding and helpfulness that an ex-partner may be able to offer you as a friend for the rest of your life. When bitterness and hatred replace love, it can be devastating to your children.

The wellsprings of your perception can be poisoned by your paranoia. "Miriam is really a bitch" becomes a self-fulfilling judgment. If your separate-self labels a person as hostile, you will treat them with hostility. And they'll probably respond with antagonism. And you then think your original judgment is confirmed by *their* hostility. But suppose you had done what you had to do—with love in your heart?

Responsibility Without Blame

You can take responsibility for your part in creating the relationship; you can take responsibility for your part of what happened in the relationship; and you can take responsibility for the part you are playing in altering the form of the relationship.

Please note again that taking responsibility is very different from blaming yourself or others. Don't get caught in the blaming trap. It's only when you keep love alive in your heart that you can use your internal wisdom to come through the separation or divorce with your self-esteem intact.

---

* Can you imagine what beneficial intentions the husband may have had behind that action? Perhaps to see himself as relieved, satisfied, effective, respected, or acknowledged? (Too bad he didn't find a more skillful way to achieve his intentions.)

Your *involvement* may be conditional, but keep your *love* unconditional. Throw someone out of your home if you must—but don't throw them out of your heart! For when you throw someone out of your heart, your mind will perceive them through distorted, addictive filters. If you hate someone, you may not even notice the cooperative things that person may say or do.

Let's look in on one of our workshops:

> There's a lot of addictive programming that is triggered by a parting—especially of a long-standing relationship. You'll have to deal with programming that you have triggered at both a conscious and unconscious level, and also with addictions that will be triggered by your partner. If your partner is not totally in agreement with altering the form of the relationship, there could be a lot of anger and frustration coming toward you. And there are sideline people—relatives, children, friends—whatever. There is a lot of stuff that comes up. Without being centered, without staying in a love space, you start bouncing off and becoming again the result of other people's spaces—as opposed to working from your own.

> So it's important that you keep your head as clear as possible so that your decisions will be based on what you want and what you're choosing to create, as opposed to an overreaction to other people's actions. So what we're saying is that if you want to be a creative cause in altering the form of your relationship, you have to keep your head clear. Otherwise you become the effect.

> You can be taking responsibility for setting it up and having initiated altering the form, and you can be going along with the agreements, but if you're not keeping your heart open, you can be thrown into confusion by your addictions—even though you've avoided blaming and taken responsibility up to a certain point. So all the way through it, you have to be working on your head. All the way through!

Using It for Growth

You will recall in Chapter 14 that we found out how to gain even when we appear to lose. We can gain in personal growth when we lose our marriage. And this means using it all for strengthening our skill in loving unconditionally. This can greatly increase our odds for a happier marriage next time.

After months of deliberation, Ralph decided to leave Heather. Heather felt desperate. She willfully did everything she could to sabotage the divorce. She refused to negotiate for win-win solutions and vehemently blamed him for the "failure" of the marriage. Ralph was determined to experience *in himself* a high level of harmony and unconditional love. It was a challenge for him.

When Heather burned all the photographs of his fishing trips, he looked for her positive intentions—which he decided were to feel acknowledged and loved. When she untruthfully told his friends and family he'd had affairs with other women, he put himself in her shoes to feel what it would be like if he were in her place. And when she took all the furniture, household items, and things he regarded as his belongings, he continued to remind himself that he would use every situation (even if painful) for his personal growth.

He often felt angry and frustrated, but he continued to work on changing his addictions to preferences as well as he could whenever they came up. Although Heather never returned his items and convinced her lawyer and the court that he shouldn't have them, Ralph came out the winner in the long run. For he knew that after this situation he could handle anything.

He was stronger, wiser, more compassionate, and more loving as a result. He'd learned the lessons his life had offered him, had passed the test, and had greatly increased his chances of creating a more enjoyable relationship in the future. He was rapidly bringing the power of unconditional love into his life!

Even if you don't think so now, there is a part of you that still feels a heart connection with this person with whom you have shared some of your life. It is possible to uncover that part inside and bring the love out of hiding. Wonderful healing in your heart can then happen. A clear perspective that is undistorted by fear or hatred is wiser and more genuinely protective to you than any addictive melodrama—or contest of me-*vs.*-them power.

21

It's Only a Melodrama— So Don't Get Caught Up in It.

When you decided to get serious about going into a relationship, you probably found lots of social approval. Most people smiled and said, "That's great!" when you told them of your plans. On the other hand, except for a few close friends, most people think they're supposed to express regret and sympathy when you are changing your involvement. So it's up to you to not feed your friends' tendencies toward condolences, blame, judgmentalness—and the illusion that your life is ruined.

Try constantly to understand your partner's basic interests and concerns. Ask them, "If you don't get what you want, what are you afraid will happen?" Keep verifying your partner's beneficial, positive intentions behind the demands by asking, "If you get what you want, how will you feel?" Try to find mutually acceptable ways so both of you can feel good about yourselves and each other.

What if you want to end your relationship and your partner is still addicted to the relationship? Or vice versa? If either happens, lovingly and patiently work with the situation—back and forth. You may have the opportunity to work on addictive demands that cause impatience or anxiety. Listen carefully to what your partner is saying to you and paraphrase it back nonjudgmentally so they feel you have heard. Clearly continue communicating how you perceive the evolving situation. Be open to looking at your own addictions that make you want out.

To Accelerate Your Growth

Be compassionate with yourself. Give yourself the patience and understanding you've often given others. Do nurturing things for yourself—just as you might arrange special activities or delights for your best friend who was trapped in an addictive snarl. (But keep working on your programming!)

Consciously look at how your mind can give you the illusion that you are not a good person. Try to look at all the should's and shouldn'ts you've accumulated in your mind about winding down a relationship. Try to notice that it's your programming that gives you guilty feelings—it's not what's happening. It's possible to go through all this and be free of guilt; it's a matter of programming.

And remember, it's OK to have addictions. Just as it's all right to create a deeper involvement in the first place, it's also your privilege to change your involvement if you feel that's what should be happening.

It's not a catastrophe—it's only a part of your journey through life. A year or so from now all this will probably look very different.

Let's listen in on a relationship workshop:

If you keep in the back of your head at all times that LOVE IS MORE IMPORTANT than anything else that is happening in your relationship, or in altering the form of it, you can come out of this whole melodrama in a love space with your partner. The love you share does not have to depend on whether you choose to be involved or to live together.

And we should look at how we have to make our involvement wrong before we can change our involvement. We rationalize to declare this thing wrong and that thing right. So in altering the form of the relationship, we get into the game of making our partner wrong so we don't have to take responsibility for choosing to alter the form. If we take that responsibility, we do not have to make our partner wrong.

And it's taking responsibility and being truthful that helps us stay in the love space if we choose to alter the form of our relationship. We can stay totally and completely in a love space with our partner throughout the whole period of adjustment. And then, perhaps, we can create a richer friendship and a more valuable relationship than we previously had.

Three Phases of Growth

People who blame other people or themselves for their experience in life are caught in a trap that bites tighter and tighter. Here are the phases that will pinpoint your steps in getting free from your self-imposed jail:

1. The Victim or Blaming Phase:
Somewhere in your early home and school upbringing and the books you've read, TV you've seen, and conversations you've had, you have almost surely been taught to blame other people for your feelings.

Blaming other people for your internal emotional experience creates the illusion that your happiness is dependent on the thoughts, feelings, and actions of other people. It seems like every other passing wave of life crashes over you and leaves you floundering—feeling like a victim. This is nonsense.

It's always your addictive demands and dysfunctional inner child programming that make you trigger the experience of unhappiness. And you needn't blame yourself. Just keep using everything for your growth.

2. Taking Responsibility Phase:

It's possible for you to go to your next step in creating a more enjoyable life when you have the insight that it's always your programming that creates your feelings and thoughts—your unhappiness or happiness. This insight gives you the energy to let go of your addictive demands—and change them to preferences.

Once you realize that your addictive demands are the immediate, practical cause of your illusion of separateness, you will begin to take responsibility for your experience. (And let me caution you once again, taking responsibility does not mean blaming yourself!) When you've had a direct "aha" experience that it's your addictive programming that makes you upset, you can begin to pick up speed in your journey of growth.

You'll find simple solutions that part of your mind knows—but which your addictive demands were blocking from your awareness. New solutions; new options; new opportunities. Your life will evolve into a new dimension, and you will meet every challenge with the insight that love is more important than almost anything else in life. You will perceive your life as a melodrama—and that it isn't serious. And at the same time you will realize that *your actions set up consequences* (either helpful or not so helpful) *that you will be dealing with in your life.*

3. Creative Cause Phase:

In this phase you realize that you generally choose what you get in life. With your partner, you co-create Act 1, Act 2, etc. of your relationship drama. You fully understand that you're not a victim and that your programming creates your experience. And you consciously focus on creatively changing your programming to give you the internal experience you want. You empower yourself as a creative cause of your experience!

From Victim to Creative Cause

June had been continually battered by verbal violence from her husband, Todd. She finally left him. It was easy for her to see herself as a victim—and her family and friends eagerly concurred. At first June loved the attention and commiseration she got from everyone. However, she increasingly noticed that continually perceiving herself as a victim wasn't helping her feelings of low self-worth and self-esteem.

She attended a support group, and through sharing and processing, she gradually began to take responsibility for how she had created her life. She saw how, through her dysfunctional inner child programming, she had invited Todd into her life. She began to notice the pattern she had unconsciously set up for attracting abusive men. Eventually, she saw more and more how she was a *creative cause* in her life. She began to change her programming so she could initiate and maintain the way she now chose to live.

What does it mean to gain a perspective of yourself as the creative cause of your life? I'd like to share with you more about what I dysfunctionally created with Bonita, my second wife. I had an addictive demand that she not be depressed one or more days every week. When my mind wanted to assign blame, I would say, "Bonita makes me unhappy when she's depressed." I placed upon her the responsibility for my enjoyment of life—and I was certain that I was right. She was doing it to me! I was stuck in the blaming, victim phase and it tore our marriage apart.

After our marriage had dissolved, I eventually escaped from the blaming phase by becoming aware of how my ego had created a stream of illusions based on my programs. It became possible for me to have the insight:

> When Bonita was depressed, I thought it meant something about me. But it was really my addictive demands and inner child programming that made me reject what she said and did when she felt depressed. I'm responsible for the resentment and frustration I felt; my own programming created my experience.

I stayed in the taking responsibility phase until the door opened for me to advance to the third phase. Then I recognized myself as a creative cause of my life experience. I could tell myself:

> I co-created the relationship by choosing to go into it. It didn't work out the way I wanted. There were lessons I hadn't learned. I've now gone beyond blaming, and I am taking responsibility for my experience. This step opens the door to begin *creatively causing my experience* by simply changing my own programming. Changing my tapes is easier (and more likely to happen) than trying to change someone to fit my demanding programming. I am empowering myself to enjoy my life!

This third phase of experiencing ourselves as the creative cause in our own lives helps us avoid resisting, fighting, blaming, criticizing, playing victim, and creating all sorts of separating experiences. We activate our inner power to be a conscious creator in our journey through life.

Your Expanded Horizons

We now have 21 guidelines that can enable our relation-*ship* to navigate through the stormy straits of life into the ocean of unconditional love. We would not want to be on a ship with an untrained navigator. Similarly, we are learning the value of giving ourselves ample personal growth training before deciding on a partner. This growth helps us steer around the hidden rocks that can wreck our relationship. We've explored seven guidelines to give us the basic skills we need to embark on our couples journey.

Once we have chosen our partner, our life together will usually give us opportunities each day to use the second set of guidelines. And we begin to enjoy the fresh air of our personal growth—and the joy of living together in loving harmony.

I hope you will never need the final seven guidelines for altering your involvement. But we all have our individual lessons to learn, and we may create the pain of breaking up a relationship in order to jolt ourselves into receiving a message our separate-self egos have repeatedly made us ignore.

After absorbing the guidelines in this book, you will be prepared to make the quantum leap from theory to practice. Only you can transform your knowledge into skill that can fully bring the power of unconditional love into your life.

You are the star in the drama of your life. The guidelines in this book may give you a lot of new options for scripting your lines!

PART IV

Loving Unconditionally

22

Reflections on Love.

What is love? How do we recognize the experience that the word "love" points to? If you have experienced the color "purple," words that describe it are not necessary. If you haven't experienced purple, words that define it are of little help. In a way, love is somewhat like explaining the sensation of purple to a blind person. Real communication would not happen.

Fortunately, when it comes to love, we are not in the situation of a blind person who has never seen purple. Some of us may keep ourselves on a love-starved diet, deficient in this important vitamin of the soul. But at some time or another, most of us have felt love—even if it was only in the womb or in infancy at our mother's breast. So let's continue our exploration of what we mean by "love."

Love Defined

We complicate our understanding of love when we mix it with other types of human experience. For example, we sometimes use the term "making love" when we really mean having sex. This blending of sexual energy and love may make it difficult to sort out exactly what the word "love" connects with in our memories. Just as water may offer us many different experiences depending on whether it is mixed with tea, coffee, or gin, so love may be experienced in many blended contexts. Nevertheless, it is possible to develop a clear idea of what *pure* love is like. So here's the best definition I can give with words:

> *To me, pure love is a heart feeling of accep-
> tance, caring, and warmth. Love is not
> action—although it can lead us to helpful
> actions. It is a heart bridge from separate-
> ness to oneness. And from this love feeling,
> our most beautiful and noble moments
> unfold.*

*Emotional acceptance is a major key in creating
the experience of love.* Remember that emotional acceptance does not exclude our working with a situation
in order to change it. It just means that the motivation
for changing it is not rooted in *addictively* trying to
alter a person's programming or behavior.

Opening Our Hearts to Love

In one of our relationship workshops with Carole
Thompson Lentz, here's how opening our hearts to
love was described:

> Love is a heart connection. As you grow more
> conscious, you'll experience that a lot more—and
> quicker, too—because your heart is open to another
> person coming in immediately. It's like right now
> we guard our heart. We have this little fort around
> our heart. And somebody has to give us a pass—
> prove their intention not to hurt us, prove that they're
> our friend, prove they're trustworthy—and they're
> into the first courtyard. We investigate them and
> interrogate them, and make sure they're loyal to us
> and nobody else. Then we'll let them in a little further.
> When you start to realize that you don't need those
> boundaries around your heart, and that only your own
> addictions can deprive you of the love in your heart,
> you start letting people in much sooner.

In Living Love, we do not experience love as a
feeling that we "should" have for ourselves and other

people. Instead, we find that love can naturally well up in our hearts and minds when we work on our addictive demands. We work on the subtle (and not so subtle) psychological expectations and desires that control our perceptions. In other words, we work on our programmed desire systems.

As we go beyond our separate-self programming, we see the world afresh. In the words of a sage, "For when a thing can no longer offend, it ceases to exist in the old way."

Our own personal journey of growth is the highest achievement that we could possibly attain. The external dramas of becoming wealthy or famous are child's play by comparison. And they do not yield the happiness and fulfillment of personal growth.

What Is Love?

We began this chapter with the question "What is love?" Like many profound questions about life, the real answer cannot be found in any book. Each person must discover it for himself or herself *inside themselves*—through their experience.

This book has given you many clues for bringing the power of unconditional love into your life. It has shown how your separate-self can kill it, and how your unified-self can awaken it. It has offered you concepts and terminology that will help you unlock its secrets. And it has given you methods you can apply in daily life situations to keep you on the trail.

And now you face the opportunity shared by all of us on earth—the personal challenge of bringing the power of unconditional love into your life.

23

Learning to Love.

When I attended Sunday school as a child, I heard such things as "... love your enemies, bless those who curse you, do good to those who hate you. ..." No one I knew seemed to actually live that way in daily life. I didn't understand that I could distinguish between a person and their programming, disliking their actions and still loving them as a human being. The idea of loving everyone seemed like pious mush—ideal but impractical.

As I got old enough to reflect on love, it seemed to me it would not be love if it applied to everyone. Love was something special that should be experienced with only a few people in my life—mainly my partner and my family. And with a partner, love was tricky and you had to make sure it wasn't infatuation or romantic love that would blow up on you.

When I was middle-aged, I woke up to my addictive demands, and my heart began to open. Over several years of intense inner work, I gradually experienced that it is possible to *love* everyone—but not to be *involved* with everyone equally.

I found that the quantity of the love experience will be many times greater with the person I live with. And the quality can grow into a deeper dimension as love develops into the experience of oneness.

I began to appreciate Christ as not only a great religious leader, but as a brilliant light in a dark world of human alienation and separateness. He opened people's hearts and inspired them when he taught "love one another," "love your neighbor as yourself," and "God is love." I began to realize that love is a central part of all religions. Unfortunately, the history of the past two millennia shows that it still can't be *taught*—and that it is still waiting to be *caught* by most of the world.

Expanding My Heart Feelings

One of the first breakthroughs in understanding how I could love everyone came as I mentally separated sexual desire from the experience of love. Since my sexual orientation is toward women, my cultural programming told me that a man should not feel love for other men, except family members. By unhooking sexual energy from love energy, I found that I could feel love for other men. And when I was mindful of this experience of love, it seemed to me that it was similar to the love I felt with a woman to whom my heart had opened. And it was so good to have at last broken through a barrier that ruled out experiencing love for half the people on this earth!

But I was still stuck in a high degree of selectivity. Just as I could create the experience of love with only a few women, I was still creating the experience of heartfelt love with only a few men. As I continued to work on my growth, I perceived how the fixed models in my head played a large part in determining whom I would let myself love and for whom I would block loving feelings.

Then it became clear that all I had to do was to sweep away these programs inside my mind to become more and more open to love. In our essence, we are all alike. It gradually dawned on me that it was possible to "love everyone unconditionally—including myself"—even though I was a long way from doing it consistently. It was just a matter of inner work.

Developing My Love

I discovered that whenever my ego expected something from my partner in return, I lost the purity of love. The magic and spontaneity did not happen when I had a bookkeeping attitude. For love cannot be like a business deal based upon barter or equal exchange. As I began to love and serve without concern for reciprocity, a loving field opened around me in which I got back much, much more than I could ever give.

My next step was to work on keeping the door of my heart from slamming shut. I noticed that this often happened when someone said or did something in the melodrama of life that did not fit my addictive programming. I found it helpful to view the acts of myself and other people as part of a soap opera in which we're just playing out the scripts in our minds. Our words and actions are not who or what we really are.

I understood that it's OK for me to throw someone out of my territory—but it is unskillful to throw anyone out of my heart. On the stage of a theater, the actors may *consciously* fight each other when the script calls for it. But it would be unfortunate if these actors were angry at each other offstage just because the play has a fight in Act 2. I play my role, and it is unskillful to identify my real self with it.

Behind all the melodrama—*here we are*. Each of us is a precious essence of humanity—and divinity. Not only are we playing in a melodrama, we're also the audience! We are each basically a conscious-awareness that is watching the entire show from the top of the cosmic mountain. All of us have known times when we've observed ourselves. This nonjudgmental awareness became a practice that gave me a larger perspective.

An Actor in the Cosmic Drama

As I viewed my life as an actor in a cosmic game, I increasingly recognized the beautiful being that had been there inside each person all along, hidden behind the melodrama of their lives. This helped me avoid addictively reacting to the thoughts and actions that people were mechanically acting out based on their programming.

Most people unconsciously identify with their set of mental habits called "personality" and "social roles." But in spite of how they look at themselves, I found that it is always possible to look beyond the surface happenings, to open my own heart to the beautiful essence inside others that is always there—just like mine.

And then came the realization that we are even more than the actors and the audience—we are each the playwright of our own adult melodrama. The tremendous opportunity we've been handed is the freedom to create and change our own scripts as we go along. Out of my desire to write a meaningful role, I arrived at the insight that one of the most socially helpful things I can do is to work on myself to love everyone unconditionally—including myself.

Growing in Love

I was inspired by what Meher Baba said about love:

Love cannot be born of mere determination, for through the exercise of will one can at best be dutiful.

One may through struggle and effort succeed in bringing his external actions into conformity with his conception of what is right, but such action is spiritually barren, without the inward beauty of love. Love has to spring spontaneously from within; it is in no way amenable to any form of inner or outer force. Love and coercion can never go together; but though love cannot be forced on anyone, it can be awakened through love itself. Love is essentially self-communicative: those who do not have it catch it from those who have it. Those who receive love from others cannot be its recipients without giving a response which, in itself, is of the nature of love. True love is unconquerable and irresistible and goes on gathering power and spreading itself, until eventually it transforms everyone whom it touches. Humanity will attain to a new mode of being through the free and unhampered interplay of pure love from heart to heart.*

Love is not only a shortcut to harmony and happiness for partners living together—it is the only way. As we create less of an experience of "me" as a separate-self, and focus more on the reality of "us" as a part of the unity of the whole world, we experience that our own lives are amplified and expanded by loving and serving others.

Unconditional Love Is the Answer

Unconditional love for all people, including ourselves, enables us to create an experience that is absolutely priceless. This treasured experience cannot be attained through any other means. Using love as the means, as well as the goal, enables us to transform daily pettiness and discontent into gratitude and awe in being alive. Unconditional love is the secret of success in the cosmic "boot camp" we call life.

* Reprinted by permission from *God to Man and Man to God* by Meher Baba, ©1975 by Adi K. Irani.

And once we understand the powers of love and decide to develop our skill in loving, the next step is to focus on the inner work. *The desire to love is, by itself, only the first step.* The ability to love everyone unconditionally, including oneself, must be developed *by practicing it with perseverance—using the situations in our lives.*

There are many approaches to personal growth—and there is a common thread running through each. However we choose to do it, the most enjoyable human lives are characterized by energy, perceptiveness, humor, insight, wisdom, happiness, purpose—and unconditional love.

These dependable satisfactions are created by loving more, demanding less, feeling the compassion of positive intentions, and realizing the basic goodness of everyone. Only this inner work opens us to the full joy of living.

By completing this book, you have taken a giant step in your personal growth. You're on your way toward bringing your life nearer to your heart's desire. And you deserve all the love and joy this boundless universe has to offer.

Our Lives Are Precious

We are all fellow passengers on Spaceship Earth. We all are more alike than different. We have many variations in age, education, nationality, race, sex, beliefs, etc. that the separate-self blows up to divide us. However, we all have a unity behind our diversity. We all have hearts that beat, we all have human feelings and emotions, and we're all trying to live the best lives we can—based on our programming. All of us are a part of the human family that originated on this globe

We have a limited life span to enjoy our lives on this earth. We're all imperfect. We all make mistakes. We all have many talents and abilities. We all have some dysfunctional programming. We all would like others to be patient, understanding, and compassionate with us. We all want to feel loved and loving—even though we may have overriding tapes that may block the love. And all of us have a basic goodness.

Inner growth leads us to deeply experience the basic goodness of us all. It enables us to create a heart that can build bridges of love to the hearts of others. We can develop the ability to take our drama less seriously and to smile at the cosmic humor of it all. We can acquire deep dedication to helping others enjoy their lives more. We can rediscover childlike wonderment and rapture with playfulness and a joy of living. And we can fulfill the purpose of our lives by throwing off the bonds of separateness to create love and oneness together.

These can be yours. Go for it!

PART V

Messages

Acknowledgments

There is no way for me to acknowledge every source of the wisdom I have tried to package into this book. In one degree or another, perhaps everyone who has lived on earth has played a part in creating the experience of human life. All of us have helped discover the lessons that our lives are offering us to create the most fulfillment and happiness.

All the quotations from our workshops are taken from a relationship training given by Carole Thompson Lentz at the Cornucopia Institute. These passages are on pages 16, 40-41, 86-87, 91, 126-127, 157-158, 162, 167, 172-173, and 182. My appreciation goes to Aura Wright for the excellent inner child workshops she has introduced into our personal growth college.

Thanks are also due to Stuart Emery and his book, *Actualizations: You Don't Have to Rehearse to Be Yourself,* which I found inspiring. I am indebted to the work of Richard Bandler and John Grinder for the concept of beneficial, positive intentions.

My heart feels deep appreciation for Ann Hauser of Love Line Books. She assisted in editing, contributed examples applying the guidelines, and joyfully typeset the entire book with my endless revisions. Dave Carrothers, Jerry Gross, and Marjorie Tully offered many helpful suggestions.

Words cannot express my appreciation and pleasure for the way Penny and I have worked together on this book. Setting forth these guidelines that we use in our marriage brought us even more into the oneness.

Ken Keyes, Jr.
Coos Bay, Oregon

Workshops for Personal Growth

You are invited to experience our loving seminars from a weekend to seven weeks at the Ken Keyes College in Coos Bay, Oregon. Many people of diverse cultures, religions, and nationalities have found our gentle workshops profoundly helpful. They particularly appreciate the supporting atmosphere, personal guidance, and hands-on experience in applying our practical techniques to their own lives. We also offer workshops in larger cities across the United States and Canada—all at nonprofit prices.

Some of our trainings are: Joy of Living; Healing Your Inner Child; Increasing Your Self-Esteem; Self-Appreciation; Finding Inner Peace; Unfinished Business: For Adult Children of Alcoholics and Dysfunctional Families; and the comprehensive TLC! (THE LIFE CHANGING Experience), which teaches the Science of Happiness. Group activities combined with individual practice provide each participant many opportunities to explore such issues as relationships, self-esteem, career, parenting, money, health, and opening up one's loving spirit. The emphasis in all the trainings is on learning how to use practical methods to open your heart to appreciate and love yourself and other people.

Many marriages have been saved and countless individuals have increased their happiness through the lasting improvement offered by these life-enriching workshops. They provide you with practical tools *you* can use to increase your insight, love, energy, and joy of living. And the skills you learn are yours to keep and use in any situation, so that your growth can continue after the training is over.

These dynamic courses include room, board, and instruction at nonprofit prices that are less than the usual cost of such workshops. They are held in an environment offering great natural beauty and recreational opportunities. Across the street from the College are public tennis courts, jogging trails, and a delightful duck pond. Nearby are many attractive beaches. Within an hour's drive there are spectacular waterfalls and the Oregon Dunes National Recreation Area. Located on scenic U.S. 101 on the Oregon coast, Coos Bay is easily accessible by car, bus, or air. We invite you to visit us soon!

For a free catalog of weekend workshops and other courses offered by the College, send your name and address to Registrar, Ken Keyes College, 790 Commercial Ave., Coos Bay, OR 97420. Without charge you will receive a quarterly catalog listing nonprofit workshops, books, audiotapes, and videotapes. If you wish more information about the trainings, you may phone the registrar at (503) 267-6412.

Ken Keyes College, Coos Bay, Oregon

Other Books by Ken

Handbook to Higher Consciousness
Ken Keyes, Jr., $6.95

Why are our lives filled with turmoil and worry? *Handbook to Higher Consciousness* presents practical methods that can help you create unconditional love and happiness in your life. Countless people have experienced a dramatic change in their lives from the time they began applying the effective techniques explained in the *Handbook*. There are over one million in print worldwide.

Handbook to Higher Consciousness: The Workbook
Ken and Penny Keyes, $5.95

Filled with three months of worksheets, this workbook is geared for the busy person. In 15 to 20 minutes a day, you can begin to apply the methods presented in *Handbook to Higher Consciousness* in your day-to-day interactions with yourself and others. Each day you are gently guided to uncover those roadblocks that are keeping you from experiencing the most enjoyable life possible. Based on years of practice by thousands of "living lovers," this workbook offers the daily practice you need to get results. It is a great way to get it working in your life!

197

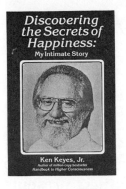

Discovering the Secrets of Happiness:
My Intimate Story

Discovering the Secrets of Happiness: My Intimate Story
Ken Keyes, Jr., $7.95

In this inspiring story, Ken shares his own journey of inner growth from being an unfulfilled man seeking happiness through money and sex to becoming a respected teacher of personal growth and world peace. Ken candidly describes his successes and failures as he recounts how he gave up a lucrative business to dedicate his life to serving others. It tells how he has successfully harnessed the power of "superlove" to create a deeply fulfilling marriage with Penny. He shows how you can enormously benefit from applying the secrets he discovered.

Gathering Power Through Insight and Love
Ken and Penny Keyes, $6.95

Here's how to do it! This outstanding book gives you detailed instructions on exactly how to develop the love inside you. Its goal is practical, how-to-do-it techniques you can use to handle upsetting situations in your life. It describes the 2-4-4 System for going from the separate-self to the unified-self: 2 Wisdom Principles, 4 Living Love Methods, and 4 Dynamic Processes. This book is based on the authors' years of leading workshops. These skills are essential for those who want the most rapid rate of personal growth using the Science of Happiness.

How to Enjoy Your Life in Spite of It All

Ken Keyes, Jr., $5.95

Learn to enjoy your life, no matter what others say or do! The Twelve Pathways explained in this book are a modern, practical condensation of thousands of years of accumulated wisdom. They help us remember when our egos blind us. Using these proven pathways will help you change your mental habits from separating, ineffective reactions to practical, loving ways for making your life work better. They promote deeper levels of insight and help increase your energy, inner peace, love, and perceptiveness in your moment-by-moment living. A must for people who are sincerely interested in their personal growth. 90,000 in print.

Your Life Is a Gift

Ken Keyes, Jr., $6.95

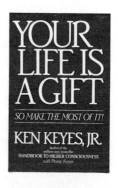

Presented in a lighthearted and delightful fashion, here is a wonderful introduction to ways you can create your own happiness. This charming book, geared toward those embarking on personal growth, shows how simple it is to experience life with joy and purpose by insightfully guiding your thoughts and actions. Every other page has an amusing and endearing drawing by Ann Hauser. Reading time is about one hour. This is a treasured gift book for everyone. 200,000 in print.

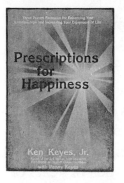

Prescriptions for Happiness
Ken Keyes, Jr., $5.95

Use these easy-to-remember secrets for happiness that work for both children and adults. Designed for busy people, this book can be absorbed in about an hour. These three simple prescriptions can work wonders in your life. They help you put more fun and aliveness into your interactions with people. They help you learn to ask for what you want with love in your heart. You can benefit from these three techniques that boost insight, love, and enjoyment in everyday situations. Some people, after reading this book, have bought out the bookstore to give copies to their friends. 159,000 in print.

Taming Your Mind
Ken Keyes, Jr., $7.95

This enjoyable classic (which has been in print for 35 years and is more relevant today than ever) shows you how to use your mind more effectively. Explains six "Tools for Thinking" that can enormously improve your success in making sound decisions, getting along with people, being more effective in business—and helping to build a better world. Written in an entertaining style with drawings by famous cartoonist Ted Key, it was adopted by two national book clubs. Over 125,000 copies in print.

Your Heart's Desire—
A Loving Relationship
Ken Keyes, Jr., $4.95

Do you want to bring the magic of enduring love into your relationship? All of us have had a taste of what heart-to-heart love is like. We cherish those times and strive to experience them continuously. Using your rich inner resources, this book can inspire you to create a more loving relationship—without your partner's having to change! It can help you to beautifully deepen the harmony, love, empathy, and trust in your relationship.

The Hundredth Monkey
Ken Keyes, Jr., Pocketbook, $2.50

There is no cure for nuclear war—ONLY PREVENTION! You are introduced to a new way of realizing your impact on the world around you—a quantum leap in consciousness. The people of our planet must use their grassroots energy to halt the suicide of the human race. You'll find here the facts about our nuclear predicament that some people don't want you to know. It gives details on our terrible killing power that could wipe out humanity. It can be read in a little over an hour. Internationally acclaimed, over one million copies have been distributed throughout the world. This dynamic little book has been translated into nine languages, including Russian.

PlanetHood

**Benjamin B. Ferencz and
Ken Keyes, Jr., Pocketbook, $2.50**

This breakthrough book, which is the sequel to *The Hundredth Monkey*, explains what must be done to give ourselves and our families a future in this scientific age. It tells how we can replace the *law of force* with the *force of law*. It explains eight ways you can personally help the world settle disputes *legally*—instead of *lethally*! Discover this workable, practical way you can play your part in bringing prosperity and permanent peace to our planet. 300,000 in print.

Meeting the Challenge

You can empower yourself to make a difference. Since your future and the life of your family may depend on rapidly replacing the law of force with the force of law, we are making *PlanetHood* available for as low as 50¢ per copy! Please buy as many copies as you can and distribute them quickly.

To help you do this, the list price of *PlanetHood* is $2.50. For only $3 postpaid, we will mail a copy of this book to any person in the world for whom you furnish the name and address. If you buy a case of 100, we will mail the case anywhere in the United States at a cost of only 70¢ per book (a total of $70 postpaid in the U.S.). If you buy 1,000 or more, they will cost only 50¢ per book (a total of $500 including shipping in the U.S.). Send orders to Ken Keyes College Bookroom, 790 Commercial Avenue, Coos Bay, OR 97420. For VISA or MasterCard orders call (503) 267-4112.

**All these books are available in bookstores
or see page 205 for order form.**

Two powerful workshops on tape!

Handbook to Higher Consciousness
Ken Keyes, Jr.

$9.95, Cassette,
approximately 1 hour

Includes a
32-page Mini-Guide to
Higher Consciousness

➤ Ken personally brings to you on audiotape his modern, practical blueprint for a life of love and happiness.

➤ Includes a 32-page Mini-Guide to Higher Consciousness that can guide you toward a vibrant, loving, happy, and fulfilled life!

➤ If you've had enough of the up-and-down roller-coastering between pleasure and pain, then you are ready to apply these step-by-step methods to improve your life while you live it!

Gathering Power Through Insight and Love
Ken and Penny Keyes

$15.95, 2 Cassettes

Includes a
48-page Workbook

➤ These dynamic cassettes are taken from the popular workshops designed by Ken and Penny Keyes.

➤ Expanding on the principles found in the *Handbook*, Ken and Penny explain and demonstrate specific techniques to help you put the Living Love Methods to work daily.

➤ Offers practical and precise ways to develop the skills that can radically improve the quality of your life.

See page 204 for ordering information.

ORDERING INFORMATION

Books

#600	$6.95	Handbook to Higher Consciousness
#670	$5.95	Handbook to Higher Consciousness: The Workbook
#665	$7.95	Discovering the Secrets of Happiness: My Intimate Story
#660	$6.95	Gathering Power Through Insight and Love
#610	$7.95	The Power of Unconditional Love: 21 Guidelines for Beginning, Improving, and Changing Your Most Meaningful Relationships
#605	$5.95	How to Enjoy Your Life in Spite of It All
#615	$6.95	Your Life Is a Gift
#620	$5.95	Prescriptions for Happiness
#630	$7.95	Taming Your Mind
#625	$4.95	Your Heart's Desire
#635	$2.50	The Hundredth Monkey
#640	$2.50	PlanetHood

Audio Cassettes

#500	$9.95	Handbook to Higher Consciousness, with a 32-page Mini-Guide
#510	$15.95	Gathering Power Through Insight and Love, two tapes with a 48-page Workbook
#114	$6.95	The Twelve Pathways and "Our Way to Happiness"
#201	$14.95	Prescriptions for Happiness, the entire book read by Ken

Music Cassettes (#109, 110, 115, 120, 125—4 for $25.00)

#109	$6.95	Ocean of Love
#110	$6.95	The Oneness Space
#115	$6.95	Open Up Your Vision
#120	$6.95	Carry the Love
#125	$6.95	The Twelve Pathways in Song
#111	$3.00	The Hundredth Monkey

Posters

#315	$3.95	The Twelve Pathways

Other

#645	$6.95	Living Love Songbook (words and music to music cassettes #109, 110, 115, and 120)

For a more complete listing of books, audio and video tapes, posters, and workshops, send for a free catalog to Ken Keyes College, 790 Commercial Avenue, Coos Bay, OR 97420, or phone 503-267-6412 or 1-800-545-7810, Monday through Friday, 9:00 a.m. to 4:30 p.m. Pacific time.

TO ORDER BOOKS AND TAPES (See pages 197 to 204.)

Qty.	Item No.	Item	Price	Amount

Please include shipping and handling charges: $1.50 first item, 50¢ for each additional item.

Subtotal	
Shipping	
TOTAL	

☐ **Yes!** Please put me on your mailing list and send me a free catalog listing workshops, books, posters, and audio and video tapes.

Ship to: (please print) _____

Address _____

City _____

State _____ Zip _____

Telephone No. ( ) _____

For ( ) VISA or ( ) MasterCard orders only:

Card # _____

Exp. Date _____ Signature: _____

Ken Keyes' books may be purchased through any bookstore. For mail order, send your check in U.S. funds or credit card information to Ken Keyes College Bookroom, Suite 610, 790 Commercial Avenue, Coos Bay, OR 97420. To order by phone with VISA or MasterCard call: (503) 267-4112, Monday through Friday, 9:00 a.m. to 4:30 p.m. Pacific time.

Index

A

"Aha" experience, xi
Acceptance
  emotional, 31
    example of, 60-61
    major key to love, 182
    OK to disagree, 60
Actions
  have consequences, 174
Addiction
  See Demands
Adler, Alfred, 20
Advice From a Failure, 21
Agapo, 4
  See Love, unconditional
Arnold, Thurman, 53

B

Barlow, Brent, 48
Beattie, Melody, 35
Behavior
  created by programming, 5-6
  not to be confused with essence, 6
  reprogramming, 6
  See Demands
Beneficial positive intentions
  See Positive intentions
Berne, Eric, 39
Blaming
  example of, 124
  phase of growth, 173-174
  responsibility without, 149-152, 166-167
  See Growth
Bradshaw On: The Family, 13
Bradshaw, John, 13, 76-77
  Bradshaw On: The Family, 13
  Healing the Shame That Binds You, 16
Brown, Scott, 67

Butterworth, Eric, 152
Buying in, 89-91

C

Caring, 48
Cause
  and effect, 31-32, 82
  creative cause phase of growth, 174-176
  erroneous, 31-32
  example of, 175-176
  how—not why, 32
  immediate, practical, 33
  infinite regress, 32
Change
  applies to everything, 34
Child
  injured, *See* Child, inner
  inner, 16-18, 34
    books recommended, 13, 16, 35
    hidden in subconscious, 34
  See Dysfunction
Choice Making: For Co-dependents, Adult Children and Spirituality Seekers, 35
Christ, 185-186
Codependency
  hidden like iceberg, 17
  See Dysfunction
Codependent No More, 35
Commitment
  don't make casually, 161-162
  example without, 48
  honoring commitments, 161-162
  love not basis for, 37, 41
  need for, 48
  three criteria for, 38-40
Communication, 48
  ask for what you want, 89-92
  asking with love, 91-92

avoid aggression or retreat, 89
builds trust, 75, 87
when separating, 155-158, 171
Compassion
definition of, 21
formulating positive intention helps, 112
leads to acceptance, 37
with yourself, 172
Computer
garbage in, garbage out, 7
Core beliefs
See Dysfunction, 17
Cosmic humor, 172, 191
Coudert, Jo, 21
Creative cause
of experience, 31, 46
phase of growth, 174-176

D

Demands, 22-35, 59-70
addictive, 23
asking without demanding, 89-92
cause misperception, 25, 64-65
cause righteousness, 26
cause unhappiness, 24, 62-65
changing to preferences, 14, 23-31, 61-70, 82-84, 99-102, 141
Compare with Preferences
create negative feelings, 24-25, 28
definition of, 23
don't work on partner's, 95-98
enemies of happiness, 64-65
example of, 7-9, 14, 25-26, 29
first wisdom principle, 28-29, 61-62
get stronger with practice, 81

identified by emotions, 23 29
not good or bad, 65
payoffs for, 65-67
example of, 66-67
penalties of, 63-65, 133-144
relation to inner child dysfunction, 34
trap of, 124
two-handed approach, 98
working on, 100-102, 142
Differences
beneficial use of, 53, 56
examples of, 54
honoring, 53-56
Discovering the Secrets of Happiness, 142
Dysfunction, 12-21
acquiring program, 16
like infection, 17
need additional help, xii-xiii
percentage of, 15
recommended books, 13, 16, 35
related to demands, 64
See Demands
ways of, 20
your adult responsibility, 18

E

Earth, planet, 131, 134, 146, 189
Ego
See Separate-self
Enoughness, 134-136
Eros, 4
Essence
of human being, 20

F

Facing Codependence, 35
First wisdom principle, 28-29
Fisher, Roger, 67
Five freedoms, 45
example when denied, 45
Freud, Sigmund, 20

Frost, Robert, xii

G

Game
    cosmic, 187-188
    use of term, 39
Gathering Power Through Insight and Love, 19, 30, 100, 157
Getting Together: Building a Relationship That Gets to Yes, 67
Gibran, Kahlil, 151
Gifts
    for growth, 123-129, 142
    give all you can afford, 119-121
    ones you can't afford example of, 49
    problems viewed as, 60
Giving
    happiness through, 131-137
God to Man and Man to God, 189
Goodness
    our basic, 7, 107, 110, 190-191
    See Positive intentions
Gorman, Paul, 136
Groups
    12-step, 19
Growth, 191
    example of, 127-128, 168-169
    life ideal for, 126-129
    messages for, 125-128
    See Preferences
    slowed by blaming, 123-125
    three factors of, 69
    use everything for, 123-129
    work on your own, 95-103

H

Handbook to Higher Consciousness, 19, 100

Handbook to Higher Consciousness: The Workbook, 100
Happiness
    cause of, 61-63
    creating, 23
    demands are enemies of, 64-65
    finding highest, 132-136
    key to, 26-27
    science of, 31
Healing the Child Within, 15
Healing the Shame That Binds You, 16
Heart
    expanding feelings of, 186-187
    opened from inside, 29
Helping others, 131-137, 189
Homo sapiens, 131
Honesty, 75-87
    builds trust, 75-76, 87
    enriches your life, 77
    example of dishonesty, 76-77
    needed when separating, 155-158
How Can I Help?, 136

I

Inferiority complex, 20
Intimacy
    ingredients for, 59
    See Love, unconditional
Involvement, 40-41
    altering, 142-146
    is conditional, 167, 185

J

Jealousy, 96-97
Joy of living, 190

K

Ken Keyes College, 195-196

L

Law
   force of, 132
Law of higher consciousness,
   xi, 3, 9, 97
Lentz, Carole Thompson
   workshop excerpts by,
   16, 40-41, 86-87, 91,
   126-127, 157-158, 162,
   167, 172-173, 182
Life
   as an adventure, 40, 53
   ideal for growth, 126-129
   purpose of, 191
   school for growth, 34, 60
   win some, lose some, 48
Life event
   definition of, 24
Limits, 49
   everyone has them, 50
Living love methods, 105
Love
   aided by example, 46-47
   awakened by love, 189
   both means and goal, 189
   conditional, 3
   deficiency of, 37
   definition of, 181-182
   discovered by experience,
   183
   distinguish from sex, 181,
   186
   for everyone, 38
   highest life enrichment,
   183
   is best for yourself, 47
   is most important, 9, 172-
   173
   must be "caught" not
   taught, xi-xii, 186
   naturally wells up, 182-
   183
   romantic, 105-106
   See Positive intentions
   See Preferences
   service through, 136
   unconditional, 3-11
     benefits of, 38
     cannot involve barter,
     187

     creates world of love,
     38
     develops compas-
     sion, 152
     example of, 5
     for yourself, 9
     helps avoid self-
     centeredness, 134
     knowing positive
     intention helps,
     110, 112
     meaning and impor-
     tance, 3-11, 189-190
     most powerful force,
     4
     necessary for health,
     10
     not indifference, 3
     OK to decrease
     involvement, 187
     OK to oppose
     actions, 6
     opens many options,
     7
     power of, 10-11, 132
     secret of success, 189
     See Demands
     separating person
     from problem, 4-5,
     8
     socially helpful, 188
     throughout divorce,
     165-169
     trusting power of, 43,
     46
     way to love uncondi-
     tionally, 5
     yields wisdom, 136
Love, Medicine & Miracles, 10

M

Male-female polarities, 120-
   121
Marriage
   making it work, 48
   monogamy, 119 120
McClure, David W., 151-152
Meher Baba, 188-189
Mellody, Pia, 35
Mental illness, 17

Mind
  how it operates, 28
  See Programming
  subconscious, 15, 17, 34-
  35
  runs one's life, 16

N

Narcissus, 9
Now moment, 15, 129

O

Oneness
  as purpose of life, 191

P

Pathways
  twelve, 101
  use of, 83, 100
Penny Keyes, 19, 86, 96-97,
  106
Perfection
  misuse of ideals of, 53
Phelps, William Lyon, 69
Philia, 4
Pollard, John K., III, 35
Positive intentions, 105-116
  always apply, 114-115
  based on desired internal
    experience, 108
  cautions about use of, 112
  definition of, 108
  distinguish from goals,
    111
  example of, 107-114
  identifying, 111
  intentions behind inten-
    tions, 113-114
  list of, 109
  purpose of, 112
  we're all similar, 115
Preferences, 22-35, 59-70
  Compare with Demands
  definition of, 24
  example of, 14, 30
  first wisdom principle, 28-
    29

four characteristics of, 30
identified by emotions, 29
needed for happiness, 24,
  27, 28, 62, 68-69
you can still be "right," 30
as a way to personal
  growth, 24
Programming
  Compare with Demands
  Compare with Preferences
  creates behavior, 5
  creates feelings, 24, 62
  creates melodrama, 171-
    178
  distinguish person from,
    5, 8
  learn about partner's, 49-
    50
  no limit to changing, 34
  three growth phases of,
    173-176
    example of, 175-176
  victim, 26
  we are not our program-
    ming, 7
  working on your own, 99
Prophet, The, 151

R

Ram Dass, 78, 136
Relationship
  aliveness in, 87
  beauty and perfection of,
    128
  dysfunctional, 13
  first with yourself, 13-21
  guidelines for ending,
    141-146
  if you must have, 13, 21
  See Positive intentions
  See Preferences
  three bases of, 48
  won't make you happy,
    59-70
Repression, 16, 80-83
Reprogramming, 80-83
  daily practice for, 99-103
Responsibility
  Compare with Blaming
  for your reaction, 62

without blaming, 149-152, 174
Right-wrong games, 45

S

Satir, Virginia, 45
Schweitzer, Albert, 133
Second wisdom principle, 106
Self-acceptance, 21
  can be easier, 16
Self-confidence, 14
Self-Parenting, 35
Self-rejection, 10, 20
Separate-self
  growing beyond, 44, 150-151
  magnifies differences, 190-191
  right-wrong games, 45
  See Demands
Sharing, 85-87
  form for, 102
  inner feelings, 100-102
Siegel, Bernie, 10
Sorokin, Pitirim A., 10
St. Francis of Assisi, 51
Suppressing, 80-83

T

Tapes
  mental, 5-6
  mind as recorder, 6
Trust
  built by communication, 75, 87
  See Honesty
Two-handed approach, 98

U

Unconditional Love
  See Love, unconditional
Unconscious
  See Mind, subconscious

Unhappiness, 22-35, 59-70
  cause of, 61-63
  See Demands
Unified-self
  benefits of, 43
  See Positive intentions
  See Preferences
Unity
  behind diversity, 190-191
  See Positive intentions
University of life, 126

V

Victim
  phase of growth, 173-176
    example of, 175-176

W

Wealth
  inner, 132-136
Well-being
  contributing to mutual, 44, 50-51
Wegscheider-Cruse, Sharon, 35
Whitfield, Charles, 15
Win-win, 155-158
  example of, 156
  technique for, 157
Work
  becoming play, 135-136

TO ORDER BOOKS AND TAPES (See pages 197 to 204.)

Qty.	Item No.	Item	Price	Amount

Please include shipping and handling charges: $1.50 first item, 50¢ for each additional item.

Subtotal	
Shipping	
TOTAL	

☐ **Yes!** Please put me on your mailing list and send me a free catalog listing workshops, books, posters, and audio and video tapes.

Ship to: (please print) _____

Address _____

City _____

State _____ Zip_____

Telephone No. ( ) _____

For ( ) VISA or ( ) MasterCard orders only:

Card # _____

Exp. Date _____ Signature: _____

Ken Keyes' books may be purchased through any book- ~e. For mail order, send your check in U.S. funds or credit ~nformation to Ken Keyes College Bookroom, Suite 610, ~mmercial Avenue, Coos Bay, OR 97420. To order by ~h VISA or MasterCard call: (503) 267-4112, Monday ~ay, 9:00 a.m. to 4:30 p.m. Pacific time.